Modern Encyclopedia of Typefaces
1960-90

Modern Encyclopedia of

Typefaces   1960-90

Compiled and edited by Lawrence W Wallis

Lund Humphries . London

First edition 1990
Published by Lund Humphries Publishers Ltd
16 Pembridge Road, London W11 3HL

British Library Cataloguing in Publication Data

Wallis, L. W. (Lawrence W)
Modern encyclopedia of typefaces 1960-90
1. Typefaces
I. Title
686.224

ISBN 0 85331 567 1

Designed by Alan Bartram
Typesetting (other than type samples) by
Nene Phototypesetters Ltd, Northampton
in Linotron Egyptian 505
Made and printed in Great Britain by
Butler & Tanner Ltd, Frome

Copyright

The typefaces shown in this book are, in the
majority of cases, copyright designs and may not be
copied without permission from the appropriate
manufacturer or agency. An index of manufacturers
and design agencies whose types appear is given on
page 189.

Publishers' acknowledgements

For the provision of typeface samples, the
publishers are indebted to many of the leading type
manufacturers and other organisations and
individuals. In particular, they would like to thank
the following for their co-operation:

Adobe Systems Incorporated
Agfa Corporation (Compugraphic Division)
AlphaOmega Typography
Alphatype Corporation
Autologic International Ltd
H Berthold AG
Bigelow & Holmes
Bitstream Inc
Esselte Letraset Ltd
Dr-Ing Rudolf Hell GmbH
International Typeface Corporation
Itek Graphix Corporation
Linotype Ltd
The Monotype Corporation plc
Purup Electronics
Scangraphic Visutek Ltd
St Bride's Printing Library
TVL Creative Services Ltd
Varityper Corporation (a Tegra company)
World Typeface Center

Contents

Acknowledgements

Compiling a book of this kind must have something in common with endeavouring to pick up mercury with a fork. It is a fluid subject that continues to unfold as one attempts to give an up to date and accurate account. In essence the material has been updated to around August 1989, but a supplement includes a number of faces issued or discovered between then and June 1990, which makes the work as current as possible.

My task has been made easier by many friends in the typographic fraternity who have unstintingly provided information and reference material when requested. Among them are the following: Richard Beer (Scangraphic), Charles Bigelow (Bigelow & Holmes), Ray Box (Autologic), Matthew Carter (Bitstream), Whedon Davis (formerly of Varityper), Bert Depamphilis (World Typeface Center), Allan Haley (International Typeface Corporation), Cynthia Hollandsworth (Agfa/Compugraphic), Jens Jeschke (Hell), René Kerfante (Monotype), Nick Landon, Phil Martin (Typesettra), Rudi Meissner (Scangraphic), Robert Norton (Digital Type Systems), David Saunders (Monotype), Alan Shelley (Linotype), Bill Wheatley (Digital Type Systems), Reg White (Berthold), and Adrian Williams. Additionally I am deeply indebted to John Taylor for orchestrating the production of the book, for editing the text, and for making the project a practical reality. He has saved me from my own carelessness on more than one occasion.

Any errors and omissions must be marked up against me, but I do hope that readers will point them out for the improvement of future editions.

L W W

Introduction

This is, first and foremost, an encyclopedia of typeface specimens of a particular period and scope. To qualify for inclusion, the typefaces had to satisfy certain criteria. They had to be available to a major composition system for continuous setting, thereby excluding most (but not all) of the designs completed for transfer lettering. They had to be released to the market by the manufacturers in or after the year 1960 and had to be new typefaces, as distinct from re-workings of older designs to suit the technical transitions from hot-metal matrix to photo-matrix, or from photo-matrix to digital type, or therefrom by conversion to any advanced form of digital encoding.

New typefaces

The description 'new typeface' is not the most felicitous or explicit, but serves as a substitute for the more controversial term 'original'. To define an 'original' typeface is fraught with difficulty and the whole concept has to be assessed within the framework of the long-established and familiar shapes of characters in the alphabet. To design a totally original typeface without the letter shapes being immediately recognisable to a reader would be a negation of the typographic art. Some might argue that cosmetic amendments to the shapes of a few characters within a chosen type family result in an original design. Others would regard that approach as an impertinence and withhold the adjective 'original' from the exercise and expect something more radical and novel. Some typefaces in this volume are genuinely fresh and a few even original, but many more reflect a strong antecedent and are distinctly derivative.

Numerous private types have been designed since 1960, such as those by Hermann Zapf for Hallmark International and for the Hunt Botanical Library, by Colin Banks and John Miles for the British Post Office and for the British Transport Board, and by Kris Holmes for the *Scientific American* magazine. As these, and typefaces like them privately commissioned for restricted use, are not accessible generally, they have been omitted from the present collection.

The significance of 1960

The year 1960 was chosen as the starting point for this study because it coincides roughly with the emergence of *commercial* phototypesetting in Europe. For example, the Printing Department of the Corporation of Glasgow installed an Intertype Fotosetter in 1956, the first successful industrial application of the new technology in the United Kingdom. Earlier flirtations with photographic composition are on record, as instanced by the Uhertype installation at the Dunstable plant of Waterlow & Sons Ltd in 1938, but this and other fledgling commercial experiments did not endure. It was not until the mid-1970s that the adoption of phototypesetting accelerated and began to overhaul hot-metal composition, following the introduction of budget-priced machinery, notably that produced by the Compugraphic Corporation in 1968.

Since 1960 the physical nature of type has altered radically, though irrespective of the reproductive technology the manufacturing process has tended to originate in the time-honoured way with the hand drawing of letters. However, nowadays the actual characters can sometimes be created at an electronic workstation with the aid of computer programs. In 1960, the hot-metal process of type composition was pre-eminent and looked unassailable. Metal types, in the form of slug lines or single sorts, were cast from molten metal forced into brass dies or 'female' matrices, containing recessed images of the characters as stamped into them from pantographically-cut 'male' steel punches. To produce a fount of hot-metal matrices cost a lot of money and necessitated protracted effort to cut the punches which represented special tooling. In the circumstances, the release of a significant typeface family was a cardinal event and a major commercial commitment and could not be undertaken in a light-hearted manner by typefounders and hot-metal composing machinery manufacturers.

Phototypesetting

With the advent of phototypesetting, the character matrix became a photographic negative in the form of a disc, grid, or filmstrip. Most photo-matrices accommodated several founts and could be produced relatively inexpensively compared to hot-metal equivalents. In essence, the drawings of characters were photographed on proprietary precision cameras into a master matrix from which contact prints were taken to yield photo-matrices for delivery to the typesetter. Undoubtedly recourse to photography facilitated the unprincipled copying or pirating of type designs with greater ease than previously. A given design could be obtained under a variety of names contrived to avoid infringement of registered trade marks, since the protection of the actual type designs themselves was impossible under copyright or intellectual property statutes. In recent years a few countries have extended legal protection to typefaces, notably France, Germany, and to some extent the United Kingdom (Copyright, Designs and Patents Act, 1988) and the geographical spread seems likely to expand.

Digital founts

In 1965, Dr-Ing Rudolf Hell GmbH released the Digiset phototypesetter, the first to utilise digitised founts for image generation on an output cathode ray tube (CRT) from which exposures through an optical system were made on to photo-sensitive materials. Digital founts were held in the computer memory as mathematical expressions and assumed an abstraction unknown to hot-metal matrices and photo-matrices. Typesetting houses received digital founts as recordings on magnetic media, such as tapes and diskettes of diverse formats and sizes. On the Digiset machine, the digital founts were stored as run-length coding. That is, the characters were dissected or analysed into fine vertical slices or run lengths and start/stop points for each line were noted in the computer memory for eventual generation on the imaging CRT as a prelude to exposure. Each run length effectively consisted of a series of light spots or pixels (picture elements), the smallest components in the construction of a digital image. Characters could have been stored as full mosaics of pixels or bitmaps, but expression as run lengths resulted in compression of the data and more frugal use of computer memory. All digitally-encoded type when in use is ultimately exploded or dilated into a bitmap for exposure, but the mathematical method of defining characters digitally has an important bearing on the quality of the final output images. By storing the characters as run lengths, the electronic scaling of the characters over a range of point sizes could only be done within severe limits and the output resolution varied to bestow inconsistent quality.

CRT technology

Digital type took a significant step forward in 1971 when the Seaco 1600 cathode ray tube phototypesetter made its appearance. It was a total failure as a machine in commercial terms, but the technical specification envisaged the use of digital founts with the outlines of the typographical characters encoded as vectors or straight-line segments. Such a technique was thrifty in terms of the occupation of computer storage, permitted virtually infinite electronic scaling over a wide span of point sizes, and preserved output quality by imaging at a constant resolution. Not until 1973, however, did the concept of outline founts achieve commercial success with the launch of the MGD Metroset cathode ray tube phototypesetter. Nevertheless, the access initially to digital type systems tended to be somewhat rarefied because of the high prices attaching to the technology and as a result photo-matrix systems continued to be dominant in the market. That imbalance began to shift in 1978 with the release of the Linotron 202. This vouchsafed the penetration of digital type into the middle and upper reaches of the market, while the introduction in 1979 of the CRTronic brought the benefits of digital type to the desktop in numerous smaller print shops. Both the machines emanated from the Linotype group of companies, and its competitors were obliged to follow suit and to switch swiftly from photo-matrix to digital technologies. Inexorably digital type has continued to grow in importance and currently is omnipotent in the field of typographical reproduction, though the exposure units or image-recording engines have moved away from CRT to laser technology.

Improvements in digital founts

Over the years the approaches to encoding the shapes of typographical characters as outlines have improved in refinement and fidelity. On the early Linotron 202 and CRTronic machines, the outlines were described as a sequence of straight-line segments or vectors. Accordingly, a curved line in a large size of type would reveal this structure as a series of 'flats' in the final photographic output. Next came enhancements in the vector program by making the straight-line segments shorter and consequently less noticeable when synthesising curved strokes in the character shapes. Eventually line and arc methods of encoding characters emerged which safeguarded veracity to the original artwork, such as that in the Varityper Comp/Edit 6400 phototypesetter employing founts developed with the Spirascan digitising process invented by Peter Purdy and Ronald McIntosh in 1979. Nowadays every digital type system has the ability to record arcs and lines faithfully, and finished pages of high-resolution composition will not betray traces of their digital origins or structure.

PostScript language

Perhaps the most common kind of digital fount encountered in the composition industry at present contains outlines of typographic characters encoded in Bezier curves to match the requirements of the PostScript page description language developed by Adobe Systems Inc and introduced in 1983. In essence a PostScript composition system consists of an electronic workstation used to prepare job files in accordance with the syntax of the language. Afterwards the job file is fed to an imaging device equipped with a PostScript interpreter or raster image processor which explodes the computer code into an image bitmap for output. There are a number of significant features that need to be understood about the PostScript page description language and many of its competitors. Most importantly it is independent of device and resolution. This means that once a job file has been completed it can be passed to any device with a PostScript interpreter, such as a plain-paper laser printer of 300 dots per inch resolution, a photographic imagesetter of varying resolutions up to over 3000 dots per inch, or to a display PostScript workstation screen modelling images at 75 to 100 dots per inch resolution. Furthermore, the PostScript language is in the public domain and accessible to any system and software developer. Previously composition languages had been proprietary and exclusive to individual manufacturers. As a result the different systems could not communicate readily with one another. Within the PostScript environment, a job file can be switched between different devices, irrespective of resolution or source of manufacture. It is a common language akin to a typographic Esperanto.

Most of the major manufacturers of typographic output devices have endorsed the PostScript language and have licensed interpreters from Adobe Systems Inc, such as Autologic, Compugraphic, Linotype, Monotype, Scangraphic, and Varityper. Others have implemented clone interpretations of the language, as with Berthold and Itek. Additionally a huge array of electronic printers with PostScript raster image processors has emerged as well, while a company of the substance of IBM has endorsed display PostScript. The ubiquity of PostScript has had a profound impact on digital type. Time was when the purchase from a supplier of a composition machine automatically secured access to a type library of similar brand. In other words, the acquisition of a Lasercomp machine, fitted with a proprietary raster image processor, pre-ordained use of Monotype digital founts. Other manufacturers' output devices were similarly twinned with their type libraries. With the widespread adoption of PostScript, a number of supply companies have developed digital type libraries compatible with the language, thereby creating a typographic universe or 'open' fount environment. Free of customary constraints, a printer, typesetter, or desktop publisher can relish the prospect of assembling the choicest and most exclusive typographic plums from diverse sources. Accordingly the Gill, Imprint, Plantin, and Rockwell families from Monotype might reside in an applications library with Garth Graphic from Agfa/Compugraphic and with Palatino and Optima from Linotype, perhaps all running on an Autologic machine. There is no need any longer to be typographically trammelled by the brand of equipment installed.

At the beginning of 1989 the PostScript language looked to be omnipotent and unassailable for encoding page descriptions, but in the middle of that year the unanimity began to crack with the announcement that Apple Computer Inc would not embrace display PostScript and instead would develop its own version of the language for modelling viewing screen images and for output printing. Furthermore, the founts were to be encoded in quadratic curves to a new TrueType format, rather than the Bezier curves of PostScript. Sun Microsystems, too, have published an F3 open fount format which has been endorsed by Berthold, Linotype, Monotype, and others. Similarly the Compugraphic Intellifont technology cannot be ignored. It seems reasonable to suppose, however, that PostScript will continue as a potent force in the industry and 'open' fount technology as a principle seems scarcely under threat.

typography   *typography*   typography
                                             typography

typography   ***typography***
                                             typography

typography   *typography*
                                             typography
                                             typography

typography   ***typography***

typography   typography   typography
typography
                                typography   typography

typography
typography   typography   typography

Samples produced on an Apple® Macintosh™ Plus and
output at 300 d.p.i. on an Apple® LaserWriter® II.

Electronic modulation of characters

In the days of hot-metal composition, the control over the actual forms of
typographic characters rested solely in the hands of the typefounder or composing
machinery manufacturer, though the arrangement and deployment of those same
characters was the responsibility of the typesetter and printer. With digital type the
same orderliness and strict division of influence does not exist. On receiving a digital
fount, the typesetter and printer has facilities within modern imagesetters to modulate
electronically the shapes and appearances of characters in several ways. The possibilities
include condensing, expanding, sloping backwards and forwards, cameoing, tinting,
patterning, outlining, contouring, rotating, shadowing, and so forth, and more than one
electronic effect can be applied to a set of characters at the same time. It goes without
saying, too, that a digital fount can be scaled dynamically in very fine increments to span
a wide range of point sizes up to poster proportions. Very occasionally a digital type style
is furnished as a couple of master founts to cover different bands of output sizes.
The PostScript language is richly endowed with typographical functions and the
accompanying specimens give some indications of the variations and effects obtainable
from a single digital type style, thereby extending the range of typographical expression
quite considerably and inexpensively. However, the ability to modulate characters
electronically to the stage of illegibility needs to be controlled by designers and machine
operators of sensitivity and taste and versed in the tenets, traditions, and disciplines
of typography. This is a matter of genuine concern nowadays because of the
democratisation of typography that has taken place which places digital founts in
the hands of the uninitiated and untrained.

Spacing and letter fitting

Another important evolution that has occurred over the years concerns the spacing or fitting of letters. In hot-metal technology, a character was fixed in space by the typefounder or composing machinery manufacturer within the confines of a metal body. Its spatial relationships with neighbouring characters were similarly predetermined. Only with the utmost difficulty could the typesetter or printer tamper with the established order by mortising juxtaposed letters; a time-consuming and crude task. By contrast, a fount of digital type can literally float in space; the typesetter or printer is able to interfere with the natural spacing built in by the supplier. Kerning and tracking programs provide this sometimes dubious facility and one must admit that the technique leads to some eyesores when overdone or clumsily executed. In this book, the alphabets are composed with the normal fittings conferred by the manufacturers.

Applications of digital type

It will be evident from earlier statements that digital type is no longer restricted to use with composition equipment. Applications range over a wide field of activities, such as video and broadcasting systems, computer-aided design systems, office systems, personal computers, and slide-making systems. In the graphic arts industry, the use of digital type can be found on WYSIWYG (What You See Is What You Get) video viewing screens of composition workstations, on electronic printers, and on imagesetters. Such varied environments suggest that type is produced and viewed under disparate conditions. Consequently, the appearance of a given type design can differ significantly depending upon the source of generation. Output resolution is an obvious point of divergence, with laser printers providing 300 to 600 dots per inch and imagesetters working broadly from 1000 to 3000 dots per inch. Another important difference springs from the technologies involved. Imagesetters expose on to photo-sensitive emulsions and rely upon complementary chemistry to develop latent images; electronic printers, on the other hand, in the main employ electrophotographic techniques which create intermediary images on a photo-conductive drum or belt for eventual transfer to plain paper with toner powders and liquids. Plain papers have rough surfaces and toner powder particles approximate in size to 8 microns at best. Such varying technical circumstances are reflected in the images resolved.

Hinting and resolution

Outline digital founts feature in all these technologies, the most severe and least propitious conditions (for hard copy products) prevailing at low resolution on plain paper. One can readily imagine that a small size of type, say 6 point, printed at 300 dots per inch, comprises relatively few pixels per character: the em quad for example would fill the space of 625 pixels. Narrower characters would be synthesised on a bed of even fewer pixels. Technology for generating from an outline a bitmap character at 6 point and 300 dots per inch resolution needs to be fairly refined. At higher resolutions, the problems diminish markedly. Adobe Systems Inc has undertaken significant research with the intent of improving the appearance of typographic characters at coarse output resolutions. Its methods have been given the arcane name of 'hinting' and the precise details remain something of a secret to most of the industry. In effect, the presence of hints in support of founts yields letters that have been regularised and 'sanitised' and regrettably on some occasions decharacterised. Hints safeguard against irregular stem weights and erratic serif shapes that are inbuilt dangers if a paucity of pixels is available to describe a character. Low-resolution applications up to 600 dots per inch benefit from the implementation of hints, but higher resolutions render them generally redundant. There are two main kinds of PostScript founts. Type 1 are data compressed (consume less computer memory) and contain hints with an Adobe encryption, while Type 3 exhibit none of these characteristics.

Leading type designers

Over the period from 1960 to 1990 the business of type design has been in a fairly robust condition with some notable work accomplished. Three men have been particularly prolific and influential in the period: two of them are German, Hermann Zapf, represented by thirteen type families in this book, and Günter Gerhard Lange, by fourteen, and the third, Adrian Frutiger, represented by twelve, is Swiss.

Hermann Zapf has arguably excelled more in the creation of serif faces than in other styles, though having made that statement one is acutely conscious of the graceful and triumphantly original Optima issued as a family between 1952 and 1955. His earliest, and ostensibly most effective, serif designs were released by Stempel and Linotype in the first half of the 1950s as Palatino, Melior, and Aldus. They have been widely copied and given 'piratical' labels. Samples of his work included in this book were undertaken for a motley band of patrons: Berthold, Hell, International Typeface Corporation (ITC), and Scangraphic. Marconi, a fount created in 1976 for Dr-Ing Rudolf Hell GmbH, was the first to be developed with the use of a computer-aided design system, an apt distinction as Hermann Zapf has consistently shown an alertness to technological progressions and an eagerness to design characters consonant with them. Perhaps inevitably, given the prodigious output, a touch of *déja vu* can be sensed in some of the later alphabets.

In contrast to Hermann Zapf, Günter Gerhard Lange has worked exclusively in the area of type design for a single employer. He has served as a vigilant and strict guardian of quality standards at H Berthold AG, where the typefaces exhibit a crisp Teutonic precision and where attention to detail has been uncompromising. Of the specimens shown in this book, a fair number have reverted to historical precedents for inspiration, as seen in fresh iterations of Baskerville, Bodoni, Caslon, Garamond, and Walbaum. His forays into the sanserif style have been nearly as satisfying, as witnessed by the workmanlike Imago family of 1982. Berthold has done much to maintain and to elevate quality levels in typography over recent years by raising the state of awareness through the issue of some tasteful publications, yet the company does not always receive the plaudits it deserves.

If Hermann Zapf is the contemporary king of 'serif-makers' then Adrian Frutiger could justifiably lay claim to a similar position of leadership in the sanserif fraternity. His memorable Univers family of alphabets, issued in the middle 1950s, became one of the most popular typefaces of the post-war period and continues to be widely used even though partially eclipsed by Helvetica. It was one of the first typefaces to be planned from the outset as a broad and unified family, rather than evolving in a haphazard manner with fresh variations added to appease market demand. More recent essays in the sanserif genre encompass Frutiger and Avenir, both issued initially by Linotype. The eponymous

Frutiger started life as lettering for signs at the then new Charles de Gaulle airport in Paris and has translated admirably into a distinguished typeface. Adrian Frutiger participated in phototypesetting at the infancy stage when drawing the Egyptienne typeface for the Photon/Lumitype system in 1960. This was marketed in France at the time by the typefoundry Deberny and Peignot. Other early skirmishes with the new technology involved creating the OCR B alphabet for machine scanning when commissioned by the European Computer Manufacturers' Association (ECMA) and working as a typographic consultant to IBM when the strike-on composer of that company was poised to cause unnecessary alarums in the composition business at the beginning of the 1960s. Adrian Frutiger is currently typographic consultant to Linotype, a successor of Hermann Zapf who previously served in the same capacity. Such professional associations have helped Linotype to assemble a fine library of typefaces and to exert profound influences on the market.

Several other designers have made handsome and enduring contributions to type design between 1960 and 1990. One such is Matthew Carter. His early work was conducted for Crosfield Electronics (erstwhile agent for Photon equipment) and for Linotype. Notable in his contribution for the latter was a series of scripts produced for the Linofilm system. His Galliard typeface, originally prepared for Linotype, has been enthusiastically endorsed by the market and gained prominence when adopted by the International Typeface Corporation. He has designed alphabets for specialised applications, exemplified by Bell Centennial for telephone directories. Currently he is a partner in Bitstream Inc, an independent digital type supply house which recently released the exclusive Charter founts by Matthew Carter.

For Berthold, Gustav Jaeger has produced a proficient stream of type designs for display and text composition. All exude a lively individualism, yet coupled with restraint to render them useful additions to the typographic armoury.

Twice in the last few years, Walter Tracy has made erudite and cogent contributions to the literature of typography with publication of the books *Letters of Credit* and *The Typographic Scene.* They derive from a lifetime of experience in the subject and some of it as a senior executive at Linotype. His type designs have been conceived for the specific purpose of newspaper typography and are thoroughly utilitarian and pragmatic. Three designs are included in this book. Maximus was produced for setting small run-on advertisements, while Modern was destined for composing the editorial pages of *The Daily Telegraph* and Times Europa for a similar application in *The Times.*

Another British designer who ought to be singled out for mention is Adrian Williams. His work is original and sensitive and is widely used, particularly the typefaces Congress and Seagull. In the Netherlands and elsewhere in Europe, the work of Gerard Unger is receiving increasing recognition and attention, and the adoption by the International Typeface Corporation of his design Flora will accelerate the process. Sadly, the former Toronto-based typographer, Les Usherwood, died prematurely, but his Caxton type design proved to be a splendid virtuoso performance. His legacy of other work for Berthold and the International Typeface Corporation has left an indelible mark on the period.

International Typeface Corporation

Formerly, the development of type designs was controlled and instigated by typefounders and composing machinery manufacturers. That situation began to change in the early 1970s, principally with the establishment of the International Typeface Corporation in New York, an agency that commissioned and created type designs for licensing to any machinery supplier that needed to deploy them. Other similar enterprises were to follow, such as the World Typeface Center, Typesettra, TypeSpectra, and Adrian Williams Design. Without doubt, the International Typeface Corporation has been a dominant and potent force in type design between 1970 and 1990. Not everybody would agree that the influence has been entirely beneficial and many would argue to the contrary. All the composing machinery manufacturers are licensees of ITC which means that the designs attain a ubiquitousness unknown to work from other eras. ITC faces tend to sport large x-heights, incorporate close character fitting, and involve extensive families: the latter has been facilitated by the availability of computer-aided design systems whereby a basic alphabet can be interpolated into a number of variations. For example, the design of a roman medium could be computer interpolated into light and bold affiliates. The most widely employed computer-aided design system in typeface production has been the Ikarus method developed by Dr Peter Karow in 1974. It serves several functions: (1) the conversion of scanned digital images to character outlines, (2) the conversion of analogue artwork to digital data, and (3) the interpolation of basic letter designs to yield a family of different weights, outlines, contours, etc. Some authorities in the subject insist that a computer-derived variant in a family lacks personality, authenticity, and kinship to the original design concept, as opposed to an artist actually drawing the style and maintaining vibrancy. Such a standpoint is extreme and much depends on the operation of the system and the style of typeface under development.

Specimens reproduced in this book

In most of the typeface specimens included in this encyclopedia, the alphabet synopses are composed in a size of 18 on 21 point and spaced to the manufacturers' standards without doctoring by kerning or tracking. Accompanying the samples is some basic information about the designs: the name, the designer, the company initiating the fount, and the year of issue. Additionally, a list of the major companies offering the face is provided, together with any alternative names noted against those of the issuing suppliers. In the main, the specimens consist of four settings in regular, regular italic, bold, and bold italic where these are available; otherwise, in most cases, the nearest equivalent styles are reproduced or in some cases the sole family variants that have been released. All other family members are simply listed for reference purposes. Completing the entry is any extraneous or peculiar data about the design which may be of interest.

A number of indexes are included at the end of the book. These are arranged according to designers, dates, and ownership rights and will facilitate ease of access to the body of typefaces using different selection criteria. The book also incorporates an index of alternative typeface names, and profiles of some fifty designers.

L W Wallis
Maulden, Bedfordshire

15

Type Encyclopedia

How to use the encyclopedia

There are 329 typefaces included in the main encyclopedia, with a further 16 faces, which came to hand in the last few weeks before publication, incorporated into the supplement which follows the principal entries on page 163. Cross-references to these supplementary faces are given at the appropriate places in the main alphabetical sequence.

Typefaces are displayed in strict alphabetical sequence except where slight variations occur for reasons of more effective page make-up. Entries contain details of typeface name, designer, date, original manufacturer or design agency, systems on which the typeface is available, and (in italics) alternative names under which it is known on different systems. A list of the weights and versions in which each face is available are also included, together with notes highlighting points of interest relating to the design.

In most cases, four weights – roman, italic, bold and bold italic, or their near equivalents – are displayed in 18-point synopses incorporating lower-case and upper-case alphabets, figures and punctuation. In the case of a very few faces, it was not possible to secure an 18-point synopsis, and rather than exclude these faces it was decided to show an alternative sample setting.

Following the displayed typefaces, there is a section devoted to designer profiles, and a bibliography.

The chronological index, index of designers, index of manufacturers and design agencies, and index of alternative typeface names at the end of the volume provide access to the main encyclopedia by a variety of useful routes.

Aachen

Colin Brignall
Letraset
1969

Adobe, Autologic, Compugraphic,
Linotype, Scangraphic
Charlemagne (Varityper)

Medium, bold

Medium version was designed by
Alan Meeks and introduced in 1977

abcdefghijklmnopqrstuvwxyz
ABCDEFGHIJKLMNOPQRSTUVWXYZ
1234567890 &?!£$.,;::

abcdefghijklmnopqrstuvwxyz
ABCDEFGHIJKLMNOPQRSTUVWXYZ
1234567890 &?!£$.,;::

Abadi

Ong Chong Wah
Monotype
1987

Extra light, extra light italic, light,
light italic, light condensed, regular,
regular italic, regular condensed,
bold, bold italic, bold condensed,
extra bold, extra bold italic, extra
bold condensed

abcdefghijklmnopqrstuvwxyz
ABCDEFGHIJKLMNOPQRSTUVWXYZ
1234567890 .,:;!?"

abcdefghijklmnopqrstuvwxyz
ABCDEFGHIJKLMNOPQRSTUVWXYZ
1234567890 .,:;!?"

abcdefghijklmnopqrstuvwxyz
ABCDEFGHIJKLMNOPQRSTUVWXYZ
1234567890 .,:;!?"

abcdefghijklmnopqrstuvwxyz
ABCDEFGHIJKLMNOPQRSTUVWXYZ
1234567890 .,:;!?"

Abel Cursive

Bernie Abel
Compugraphic
1974

One weight only

abcdefghijklmnopqrstuvwxyz
ABCDEFGHIJKLMNOPQRSTUVWXYZ
1234567890 &

Accolade

Chew Loon Ng
Fonts/Ingrama SA
1979

Compugraphic, Scangraphic

Light, light italic, medium, bold

abcdefghijklmnopqrstuvwxyz
ABCDEFGHJKLMNOPQRSTUVWXYZ
1234567890 &£$.,:;!?''

abcdefghijklmnopqrstuvwxyz
ABCDEFGHJKLMNOPQRSTUVWXYZ
1234567890 &£$.,:;!?''

abcdefghijklmnopqrstuvwxyz
ABCDEFGHJKLMNOPQRSTUVWXYZ
1234567890 &£$.,:;!?''

Administer

Leslie Usherwood
Typesettra
1980

Compugraphic

Light, light italic, light condensed, light condensed italic, book, book italic, book condensed, book condensed italic, bold, bold condensed

Compugraphic adopted the face in 1982

abcdefghijklmnopqrstuvwxyz
ABCDEFGHIJKLMNOPQRSTUVWXYZ
1234567890 &

abcdefghijklmnopqrstuvwxyz
ABCDEFGHIJKLMNOPQRSTUVWXYZ
1234567890 &

abcdefghijklmnopqrstuvwxyz
ABCDEFGHIJKLMNOPQRSTUVWXYZ
1234567890 &

abcdefghijklmnopqrstuvwxyz
ABCDEFGHIJKLMNOPQRSTUVWXYZ
1234567890 &

Adroit

Phil Martin
TypeSpectra
1981

Autologic, Compugraphic, Linotype

Light, light italic, medium, medium italic, bold

abcdefghijklmnopqrstuvwxyz
ABCDEFGHIJKLMNOPQRSTUVWXYZ
1234567890 &£.,:;!?"

abcdefghijklmnopqrstuvwxyz
ABCDEFGHIJKLMNOPQRSTUVWXYZ
1234567890 &£.,:;!?"

abcdefghijklmnopqrstuvwxyz
ABCDEFGHIJKLMNOPQRSTUVWXYZ
1234567890 &£.,:;!?"

abcdefghijklmnopqrstuvwxyz
ABCDEFGHIJKLMNOPQRSTUVWXYZ
1234567890 &£.,:;!?"

AG Buch Stencil

Günter Gerhard Lange
Berthold
1985

One weight only

abcdefghijklmnopqrstuvwxyz
ABCDEFGHIJKLMNOPQRSTUVWXYZ
1234567890 &£$.,:;!?"

AG Old Face

Günter Gerhard Lange
Berthold
1984

Regular, medium, bold, outline, bold outline, shaded

abcdefghijklmnopqrstuvwxyz
ABCDEFGHIJKLMNOPQRSTUVWXYZ
1234567890 &£$.,:;!?"

abcdefghijklmnopqrstuvwxyz
ABCDEFGHIJKLMNOPQRSTUVWXYZ
1234567890 &£$.,:;!?"

For **Agora** see Supplement

AG Schulbuch

Staff designers
Berthold
1983

Regular, medium

abcdefghijklmnopqrstuvwxyz
ABCDEFGHJJKLMNOPQRSTUVWXYZ
1234567890 &£$.,!?"

**abcdefghijklmnopqrstuvwxyz
ABCDEFGHJJKLMNOPQRSTUVWXYZ
1234567890 &£$.,!?"**

Aja

Gustav Jaeger
Berthold
1981

One weight only

abcdefghijklmnopqrstuvwxyz
ABCDEFGHIJKLMNOPQRSTUVWXYZ
1234567890   &£$.,:;!?"

Albertina

Chris Brand
Monotype
1964

Regular, regular italic

Second typeface commissioned
specially for phototypesetting by
Monotype. It was first used in 1966
for a catalogue of the work of
Stanley Morison exhibited at the
Albertina, the Royal Library in
Brussels

abcdefghijklmnopqrstuvwxyz
ABCDEFGHIJKLMNOPQRSTUVWXYZ
1234567890 .,:;!?"

abcdefghijklmnopqrstuvwxyz
ABCDEFGHIJKLMNOPQRSTUVWXYZ
1234567890 .,:;!?"

Allan

Valdimir Andrich
Alphatype
1978

Regular, regular italic, bold, bold italic

abcdefghijklmnopqrstuvwxyz
ABCDEFGHIJKLMNOPQRSTUVWXYZ
1234567890 &£$.,:;!?''

abcdefghijklmnopqrstuvwxyz
ABCDEFGHIJKLMNOPQRSTUVWXYZ
1234567890 &£$.,:;!?''

abcdefghijklmnopqrstuvwxyz
ABCDEFGHIJKLMNOPQRSTUVWXYZ
1234567890 &£$.,:;!?''

abcdefghijklmnopqrstuvwxyz
ABCDEFGHIJKLMNOPQRSTUVWXYZ
1234567890 &£$.,:;!?''

Americana

Richard Isbell
American Type Founders
1965

Adobe, Berthold, Linotype, Monotype, Scangraphic
Freedom (Autologic)
Flareserif 721 (Bitstream)
American Classic (Compugraphic)
AM (Itek)
Colonial (Varityper)

Light, light italic, regular, regular italic, regular condensed, regular condensed italic, bold, bold condensed, extra bold, extra bold condensed, outline

abcdefghijklmnopqrstuvwxyz
ABCDEFGHIJKLMNOPQRSTUVWXYZ
1234567890 &£$.,:;!?"

abcdefghijklmnopqrstuvwxyz
ABCDEFGHIJKLMNOPQRSTUVWXYZ
1234567890 &£$.,:;!?"

abcdefghijklmnopqrstuvwxyz
ABCDEFGHIJKLMNOPQRSTUVWXYZ
1234567890 &£$.,:;!?"

American Gothic

Vladimir Andrich
Alphatype
1967

Autologic

Light, light italic, medium, medium italic, bold

abcdefghijklmnopqrstuvwxyz
ABCDEFGHIJKLMNOPQRSTUVWXYZ
1234567890 &£$.,:;!?"

abcdefghijklmnopqrstuvwxyz
ABCDEFGHIJKLMNOPQRSTUVWXYZ
1234567890 &£$.,:;!?"

abcdefghijklmnopqrstuvwxyz
ABCDEFGHIJKLMNOPQRSTUVWXYZ
1234567890 &£$.,:;!?"

abcdefghijklmnopqrstuvwxyz
ABCDEFGHIJKLMNOPQRSTUVWXYZ
1234567890 &£$.,:;!?"

ITC American Typewriter

Joel Kadan
International Typeface Corporation
1974

Adobe, Autologic, Berthold, Compugraphic, Hell, Linotype, Monotype, Scangraphic, Varityper
Typewriter 911 (Bitstream)
AT (Itek)

Light, light italic, medium, medium italic, bold, bold italic, light condensed, medium condensed, bold condensed

Joel Kadan designed the light and medium styles; Tony Stan the corresponding bold; and Ed Benguiat was reponsible for the italics released in 1989

abcdefghijklmnopqrstuvwxyz
ABCDEFGHIJKLMNOPQRSTUVWXYZ
1234567890 &£$.,:;!?"

abcdefghijklmnopqrstuvwxyz
ABCDEFGHIJKLMNOPQRSTUVWXYZ
1234567890 1234567890 &£$.,:;!?"

abcdefghijklmnopqrstuvwxyz
ABCDEFGHIJKLMNOPQRSTUVWXYZ
1234567890 &£$.,:;!?"

abcdefghijklmnopqrstuvwxyz
ABCDEFGHIJKLMNOPQRSTUVWXYZ
1234567890 1234567890 &£$.,:;!?"

Bitstream Amerigo

Gerard Unger
Bitstream
1987

Regular, regular italic, medium,
medium italic, bold, bold italic

abcdefghijklmnopqrstuvwxyz
ABCDEFGHIJKLMNOPQRSTUVWXYZ
1234567890 &£$.,:;!?"

abcdefghijklmnopqrstuvwxyz
ABCDEFGHIJKLMNOPQRSTUVWXYZ
1234567890 &£$.,:;!?"

abcdefghijklmnopqrstuvwxyz
ABCDEFGHIJKLMNOPQRSTUVWXYZ
1234567890 &£$.,:;!?"

abcdefghijklmnopqrstuvwxyz
ABCDEFGHIJKLMNOPQRSTUVWXYZ
1234567890 &£$.,:;!?"

Antique Olive

Roger Excoffon
Olive
1962

Berthold, Compugraphic, Linotype,
Monotype, Scangraphic
Oliva (Autologic)
Incised 901 (Bitstream)
AO (Itek)
Olive (Varityper)

Light, regular, regular italic,
medium, medium condensed, bold,
bold condensed, compact, nord,
nord italic, extended.

Antique is the French term for
sanserif

abcdefghijklmnopqrstuvwxyz
ABCDEFGHIJKLMNOPQRSTUVWXYZ
1234567890 &£$.,!?"

abcdefghijklmnopqrstuvwxyz
ABCDEFGHIJKLMNOPQRSTUVWXYZ
1234567890 &£$.,!?"

abcdefghijklmnopqrstuvwxyz
ABCDEFGHIJKLMNOPQRSTUVWXYZ
1234567890 &£$.,!?"

abcdefghijklmnopqrstuvwxyz
ABCDEFGHIJKLMNOPQRSTUVWXYZ
1234567890 &£$.,!?"

For **Amigo** see Supplement

Apollo

Adrian Frutiger
Monotype
1964

Regular, regular italic, semi bold

First typeface produced specially by
Monotype for phototypesetting

abcdefghijklmnopqrstuvwxyz
ABCDEFGHIJKLMNOPQRSTUVWXYZ
1234567890 .,:;!?''

abcdefghijklmnopqrstuvwxyz
ABCDEFGHIJKLMNOPQRSTUVWXYZ
1234567890 .,:;!?''

abcdefghijklmnopqrstuvwxyz
ABCDEFGHIJKLMNOPQRSTUVWXYZ
1234567890 .,:;!?''

Arial

Staff designers
Monotype
1988

Light, regular, regular italic, bold,
bold italic

Characters have comparable widths
to those in the PostScript version of
Helvetica

abcdefghijklmnopqrstuvwxyz
ABCDEFGHIJKLMNOPQRSTUVWXYZ
1234567890 .,:;!?"

abcdefghijklmnopqrstuvwxyz
ABCDEFGHIJKLMNOPQRSTUVWXYZ
1234567890 .,:;!?"

abcdefghijklmnopqrstuvwxyz
ABCDEFGHIJKLMNOPQRSTUVWXYZ
1234567890 .,:;!?"

abcdefghijklmnopqrstuvwxyz
ABCDEFGHIJKLMNOPQRSTUVWXYZ
1234567890 .,:;!?"

For **Arbiter** see Supplement   For **Arena** see page 29

Aurelia

Hermann Zapf
Hell
1985

Light, light italic, book, book italic, bold

Work began on this design in 1979

abcdefghijklmnopqrstuvwxyz
ABCDEFGHIJKLMNOPQRSTUVWXYZ
1234567890 1234567890 &£$.,:;!?"

abcdefghijklmnopqrstuvwxyz
ABCDEFGHIJKLMNOPQRSTUVWXYZ
1234567890 1234567890 &£$.,:;!?"

abcdefghijklmnopqrstuvwxyz
ABCDEFGHIJKLMNOPQRSTUVWXYZ
1234567890 1234567890 &£$.,:;!?"

abcdefghijklmnopqrstuvwxyz
ABCDEFGHIJKLMNOPQRSTUVWXYZ
1234567890 1234567890 &£$.,:;!?"

Auriga

Matthew Carter
Linotype (Mergenthaler)
1965

Riga (Autologic)

Medium, medium italic, bold

abcdefghijklmnopqrstuvwxyz
ABCDEFGHIJKLMNOPQRSTUVWXYZ
1234567890 &£$.,:;!?"

abcdefghijklmnopqrstuvwxyz
ABCDEFGHIJKLMNOPQRSTUVWXYZ
1234567890 &£$.,:;!?"

abcdefghijklmnopqrstuvwxyz
ABCDEFGHIJKLMNOPQRSTUVWXYZ
1234567890 &£$.,:;!?"

Aurora

Jackson Burke
Linotype (Mergenthaler)
1960

News 706 (Bitstream)
News No.2 and *News No. 12*
(Compugraphic)
Empira (Varityper)

Regular, regular italic, bold

Newspaper face introduced initially
for teletypesetting by the Canadian
news agencies

abcdefghijklmnopqrstuvwxyz
ABCDEFGHIJKLMNOPQRSTUVWXYZ
1234567890 &£$.,:;!?''

abcdefghijklmnopqrstuvwxyz
ABCDEFGHIJKLMNOPQRSTUVWXYZ
1234567890 &£$.,:;!?''

abcdefghijklmnopqrstuvwxyz
ABCDEFGHIJKLMNOPQRSTUVWXYZ
1234567890 &£$.,:;!?''

ITC Avant Garde Gothic

Herb Lubalin and Tom Carnase
International Typeface Corporation
1970

Adobe, Autologic, Berthold,
Compugraphic, Hell, Linotype,
Monotype, Scangraphic, Varityper
Geometric 711 (Bitstream)
AG (Itek)

Extra light, extra light oblique,
book, book oblique, medium,
medium oblique, demi, demi
oblique, bold, bold oblique, book
condensed, medium condensed,
demi condensed, bold condensed

Design occurred in embryo as a
masthead logotype for the magazine
Avant Garde. Ed Benguiat drew the
Avant Garde Condensed styles in
1974 with the Avant Garde Obliques
following in 1977 from the hands of
André Gürtler, Christian Mengelt,
and Erich Gschwind

abcdefghijklmnopqrstuvwxyz
ABCDEFGHIJKLMNOPQRSTUVWXYZ
1234567890 &£$.,:;!?ˇ

abcdefghijklmnopqrstuvwxyz
ABCDEFGHIJKLMNOPQRSTUVWXYZ
1234567890 &£$.,:;!?ˇ

abcdefghijklmnopqrstuvwxyz
ABCDEFGHIJKLMNOPQRSTUVWXYZ
1234567890 &£$.,:;!?''

abcdefghijklmnopqrstuvwxyz
ABCDEFGHIJKLMNOPQRSTUVWXYZ
1234567890 &£$.,:;!?''

Arena (now called Stadia)

Neville Brody
Linotype
1989

Roman

Designed for *Arena* magazine launched in 1986. Suitable for text and display composition

abcdefghijklmnopqrstuvwxyz
ABCDEFGHIJKLMNOPQRSTUVWXYZ
1234567890 &£$.,:;!?"

Avenir

Adrian Frutiger
Linotype
1988

Adobe

Light, book, regular, medium, heavy, black

Sloped equivalents of the various romans are achieved by electronic slanting on a digital phototypesetter

abcdefghijklmnopqrstuvwxyz
ABCDEFGHIJKLMNOPQRSTUVWXYZ
1234567890 &£$.,:;!?''

abcdefghijklmnopqrstuvwxyz
ABCDEFGHIJKLMNOPQRSTUVWXYZ
1234567890 &£$.,:;!?''

ITC Barcelona

Edward Benguiat
International Typeface Corporation
1981

Autologic, Berthold, Compugraphic, Linotype, Scangraphic, Varityper

Book, book italic, medium, medium italic, bold, bold italic, heavy, heavy italic

abcdefghijklmnopqrstuvwxyz
ABCDEFGHIJKLMNOPQRSTUVWXYZ
1234567890 &£$.,:;!?"

abcdefghijklmnopqrstuvwxyz
ABCDEFGHIJKLMNOPQRSTUVWXYZ
1234567890 &£$.,:;!?"

abcdefghijklmnopqrstuvwxyz
ABCDEFGHIJKLMNOPQRSTUVWXYZ
1234567890 &£$.,:;!?"

abcdefghijklmnopqrstuvwxyz
ABCDEFGHIJKLMNOPQRSTUVWXYZ
1234567890 &£$.,:;!?"

For **Avanti** see page 41   For **Avantis** see Supplement

Barmen

Hans Reichel
Berthold
1983

Regular, medium, bold, extra bold

abcdefghijklmnopqrstuvwxyz
ABCDEFGHIJKLMNOPQRSTUVWXYZ
1234567890 &£$.,:;!?''

abcdefghijklmnopqrstuvwxyz
ABCDEFGHIJKLMNOPQRSTUVWXYZ
1234567890 &£$.,:;!?''

Basilia

André Gürtler
Haas
1978

Autologic, Linotype, Scangraphic

Light, light italic, medium, medium italic, bold, bold italic, black, black italic

abcdefghijklmnopqrstuvwxyz
ABCDEFGHIJKLMNOPQRSTUVWXYZ
1234567890 &£$.,:;!?''

abcdefghijklmnopqrstuvwxyz
ABCDEFGHIJKLMNOPQRSTUVWXYZ
1234567890 &£$.,:;!?'

abcdefghijklmnopqrstuvwxyz
ABCDEFGHIJKLMNOPQRSTUVWXYZ
1234567890 &£$.,:;!?''

abcdefghijklmnopqrstuvwxyz
ABCDEFGHIJKLMNOPQRSTUVWXYZ
1234567890 &£$.,:;!?''

Baskerville Book

Günter Gerhard Lange
Berthold
1980

Regular, regular italic, medium,
medium italic

abcdefghijklmnopqrstuvwxyz
ABCDEFGHIJKLMNOPQRSTUVWXYZ
1234567890 1234567890 &£$.,:;!?""

abcdefghijklmnopqrstuvwxyz
ABCDEFGHIJKLMNOPQRSTUVWXYZ
1234567890 &£$.,:;!?""

abcdefghijklmnopqrstuvwxyz
ABCDEFGHIJKLMNOPQRSTUVWXYZ
1234567890 &£$.,:;!?""

abcdefghijklmnopqrstuvwxyz
ABCDEFGHIJKLMNOPQRSTUVWXYZ
1234567890 &£$.,:;!?""

ITC Bauhaus

Edward Benguiat and Victor Caruso
International Typeface Corporation
1975

Adobe, Autologic, Berthold,
Compugraphic, Hell, Linotype,
Monotype, Scangraphic, Varityper
Geometric 752 (Bitstream)
BH (Itek)

Light, medium, demi, bold, heavy,
heavy outline

Based on a single-alphabet design
by Herbert Bayer in 1925 which
discarded capital letters: an
eccentricity not perpetuated in the
ITC derivative

abcdefghijklmnopqrstuvwxyz
ABCDEFGHIJKLMNOPQRSTUVWXYZ
1234567890 &£$.,:;!?"

abcdefghijklmnopqrstuvwxyz
ABCDEFGHIJKLMNOPQRSTUVWXYZ
1234567890 &£$.,:;!?"

Beatrice Script

Vladimir Andrich
Alphatype
1982

One weight only

abcdefghijklmnopqrstuvwxyz abcdefghijklmnopqrstuvwxyz
ABCDEFGHIJKLMNOPQRSTUVWXYZ
1234567890 &£$.,:;!?"" st nd rd th Mr Ms Mrs

Bell Centennial

Matthew Carter
Public Domain
1978

Monotype, Varityper
Gothic 762 (Bitstream)

Name/Number, Address, Sub
Caption, Bold Listing

Designed for setting the telephone
directories of the American
Telephone & Telegraph (AT&T)
company by high-speed digital CRT
techniques. It was issued in the
centenary year of the Bell
Directories. Close liaison existed
between the staff of AT&T and the
designer during development of the
face

abcdefghijklmnopqrstuvwxyz
ABCDEFGHIJKLMNOPQRSTUVWXYZ
1234567890 &'.,:;!?"

abcdefghijklmnopqrstuvwxyz
ABCDEFGHIJKLMNOPQRSTUVWXYZ
1234567890 &'.,:'''''

abcdefghijklmnopqrstuvwxyz
ABCDEFGHIJKLMNOPQRSTUVWXYZ
1234567890 &'.,:;'''''

ABCDEFGHIJKLMNOPQRSTUVWXYZ
1234567890 &'.,:;'''''

Bellevue

Gustav Jaeger
Berthold
1986

One weight only

abcdefghijklmnopqrstuvwxyz
ABCDEFGHIJKLMNOPQRSTUVWXYZ
1234567890&£$.,!?"

Belwe

Georg Belwe
Schelter & Giesecke
1913

Adobe, Autologic, Compugraphic,
Scangraphic, Varityper

Light, light italic, medium, bold,
condensed, inline

Revived by Letraset in 1976 through
the hands of Alan Meeks. Schelter &
Giesecke is now nationalised in East
Germany under the name Typoart

abcdefghijklmnopqrstuvwxyz
ABCDEFGHIJKLMNOPQRSTUVWXYZ
1234567890 &£$.,:;!?"

abcdefghijklmnopqrstuvwxyz
ABCDEFGHIJKLMNOPQRSTUVWXYZ
1234567890 &£$.,:;!?"

ITC Benguiat

Edward Benguiat
International Typeface Corporation
1978

Adobe, Autologic, Berthold,
Compugraphic, Hell, Linotype,
Monotype, Scangraphic, Varityper
Revival 832 (Bitstream)
BG (Itek)

Book, book italic, medium, medium
italic, bold, bold italic, book
condensed, book condensed italic,
medium condensed, medium
condensed italic, bold condensed,
bold condensed italic

Condensed styles were added in
1979

abcdefghijklmnopqrstuvwxyz
ABCDEFGHIJKLMNOPQRSTUVWXYZ
1234567890 &£$.,:;!?ˇ

abcdefghijklmnopqrstuvwxyz
ABCDEFGHIJKLMNOPQRSTUVWXYZ
1234567890 &£$.,:;!?ˇ

abcdefghijklmnopqrstuvwxyz
ABCDEFGHIJKLMNOPQRSTUVWXYZ
1234567890 &£$.,:;!?ˇ

abcdefghijklmnopqrstuvwxyz
ABCDEFGHIJKLMNOPQRSTUVWXYZ
1234567890 &£$.,:;!?ˇ

ITC Benguiat Gothic

Edward Benguiat
International Typeface Corporation
1979

Autologic, Berthold, Compugraphic,
Hell, Linotype, Monotype,
Scangraphic, Varityper
Informal 851 (Bitstream)
BT (Itek)

Book, book italic, medium, medium
italic, bold, bold italic, heavy, heavy
italic

abcdefghijklmnopqrstuvwxyz
ABCDEFGHIJKLMNOPQRSTUVWXYZ
1234567890 &£$.,:;!?ˇ

abcdefghijklmnopqrstuvwxyz
ABCDEFGHIJKLMNOPQRSTUVWXYZ
1234567890 &£$.,:;!?ˇ

abcdefghijklmnopqrstuvwxyz
ABCDEFGHIJKLMNOPQRSTUVWXYZ
1234567890 &£$.,:;!?ˇ

abcdefghijklmnopqrstuvwxyz
ABCDEFGHIJKLMNOPQRSTUVWXYZ
1234567890 &£$.,:;!?ˇ

ITC Berkeley Old Style

Tony Stan
International Typeface Corporation
1983

Autologic, Berthold, Compugraphic, Linotype, Monotype, Scangraphic, Varityper
Venetian 519 (Bitstream)
BY (Itek)

Book, book italic, medium, medium italic, bold, bold italic, black, black italic

Based on University of California Old Style designed as a private type by Frederic W Goudy in 1938 and first used in 1940; the face became popularly known as Californian in 1956 when released by Lanston Monotype

abcdefghijklmnopqrstuvwxyz
ABCDEFGHIJKLMNOPQRSTUVWXYZ
1234567890 &£$.,:;!?''

abcdefghijklmnopqrstuvwxyz
ABCDEFGHIJKLMNOPQRSTUVWXYZ
1234567890 &£$.,:;!?''

abcdefghijklmnopqrstuvwxyz
ABCDEFGHIJKLMNOPQRSTUVWXYZ
1234567890 &£$.,:;!?''

abcdefghijklmnopqrstuvwxyz
ABCDEFGHIJKLMNOPQRSTUVWXYZ
1234567890 &£$.,:;!?''

Berliner Grotesk

Erik Spiekermann
Berthold
1979

Light, medium

Based on an original design of 1913 called Hausschnitt

abcdefghijklmnopqrstuvwxyz
ABCDEFGHIJKLMNOPQRSTUVWXYZ
1234567890 &£$.,:;!?''

abcdefghijklmnopqrstuvwxyz
ABCDEFGHIJKLMNOPQRSTUVWXYZ
1234567890 &£$.,:;!?''

Itek Blackletter

E Strohm
Itek
1978

One weight only

abcdefghijklmnopqrstuvwxyz
ABCDEFGHIJKLMNOPQRSTUVWXYZ
1234567890 &£$.,:;!?''

Berthold Script

Günter Gerhard Lange
Berthold
1977

Regular, medium

abcdefghijklmnopqrstuvwxyz
ABCDEFGHIJKLMNOP
QRSTUVWXYZ
1234567890 &£$.,:;!?"

abcdefghijklmnopqrstuvwxyz
ABCDEFGHIJKLMNOP
QRSTUVWXYZ
1234567890 &£$.,:;!?"

Black White

Ferdinay Duman
Hell
1989

Regular, headline, laser, outline,
outline laser

ABCDEFGHIJKLMNOPQRSTUVWXYZ
ABCDEFGHIJKLMNOPQRSTUVWXYZ
1234567890 &£$.,:;!?"

ABCDEFGHIJKLMNOPQRSTUVWXYZ
ABCDEFGHIJKLMNOPQRSTUVWXYZ
1234567890 &£$.,:;!?"

ABCDEFGHIJKLMNOPQRSTUVWXYZ
ABCDEFGHIJKLMNOPQRSTUVWXYZ
1234567890 &£$.,:;!?"

ABCDEFGHIJKLMNOPQRSTUVWXYZ
ABCDEFGHIJKLMNOPQRSTUVWXYZ
1234567890 &£$.,:;!?"

Bluejack

Phil Martin
Alphabet Innovations
1974

Linotype

Light, light italic, medium, bold,
extra bold, black, open, shade

abcdefghijklmnopqrstuvwxyz
ABCDEFGHIJKLMNOPQRSTUVWXYZ
1234567890 &£$.,:;!?"

abcdefghijklmnopqrstuvwxyz
ABCDEFGHIJKLMNOPQRSTUVWXYZ
1234567890 &£$.,:;!?"

abcdefghijklmnopqrstuvwxyz
ABCDEFGHIJKLMNOPQRSTUVWXYZ
1234567890 &£$.,:;!?"

abcdefghijklmnopqrstuvwxyz
ABCDEFGHIJKLMNOPQRSTUVWXYZ
1234567890 &£$.,:;!?"

Bodoni Old Face

Günter Gerhard Lange
Berthold
1983

Regular, regular italic, medium,
medium italic, bold, bold italic

Introduced at the Imprinta
exhibition in Dusseldorf and used
for labelling the Berthold stand

abcdefghijklmnopqrstuvwxyz
ABCDEFGHIJKLMNOPQRSTUVWXYZ
1234567890 1234567890 &£$.,:;!?"

abcdefghijklmnopqrstuvwxyz
ABCDEFGHIJKLMNOPQRSTUVWXYZ
1234567890 1234567890 &£$.,:;!?"

abcdefghijklmnopqrstuvwxyz
ABCDEFGHIJKLMNOPQRSTUVWXYZ
1234567890 &£$.,:;!?"

abcdefghijklmnopqrstuvwxyz
ABCDEFGHIJKLMNOPQRSTUVWXYZ
1234567890 &£$.,:;!?"

Itek Bookface

David Kindersley
Itek
1976

Medium, medium italic, bold

abcdefghijklmnopqrstuvwxyz
ABCDEFGHIJKLMNOPQRSTUVWXYZ
1234567890 &£$.,:;!?''

abcdefghijklmnopqrstuvwxyz
ABCDEFGHIJKLMNOPQRSTUVWXYZ
1234567890 &£$.,:;!?''

abcdefghijklmnopqrstuvwxyz
ABCDEFGHIJKLMNOPQRSTUVWXYZ
1234567890 &£$.,:;!?''

ITC Bookman

Edward Benguiat
International Typeface Corporation
1975

Adobe, Autologic, Berthold,
Compugraphic, Hell, Linotype,
Monotype, Scangraphic, Varityper
Revival 711 (Bitstream)
BM (Itek)

Light, light italic, medium, medium
italic, demi, demi italic, bold, bold
italic, outline

Originally cut as a bold complement
to the Old Style design of the Miller
& Richard typefoundry

abcdefghijklmnopqrstuvwxyz
ABCDEFGHIJKLMNOPQRSTUVWXYZ
1234567890 &£$.,:;!?''

abcdefghijklmnopqrstuvwxyz
ABCDEFGHIJKLMNOPQRSTUVWXYZ
1234567890 &£$.,:;!?''

abcdefghijklmnopqrstuvwxyz
ABCDEFGHIJKLMNOPQRSTUVWXYZ
1234567890 &£$.,:;!?''

abcdefghijklmnopqrstuvwxyz
ABCDEFGHIJKLMNOPQRSTUVWXYZ
1234567890 &£$.,:;!?''

Boton

Albert Boton
Berthold
1986

Light, light italic, regular, regular
italic, medium, medium italic, bold,
bold italic

abcdefghijklmnopqrstuvwxyz
ABCDEFGHIJKLMNOPQRSTUVWXYZ
1234567890 &£$.,:;!?''

abcdefghijklmnopqrstuvwxyz
ABCDEFGHIJKLMNOPQRSTUVWXYZ
1234567890 &£$.,:;!?''

abcdefghijklmnopqrstuvwxyz
ABCDEFGHIJKLMNOPQRSTUVWXYZ
1234567890 &£$.,:;!?''

abcdefghijklmnopqrstuvwxyz
ABCDEFGHIJKLMNOPQRSTUVWXYZ
1234567890 &£$.,:;!?''

Bramley

Alan Meeks
Letraset
1980

Berthold, Compugraphic, Linotype,
Scangraphic, Varityper

Light, medium, bold, bold
condensed, extra bold

abcdefghijklmnopqrstuvwxyz
ABCDEFGHIJKLMNOPQRSTUVWXYZ
1234567890 &?!£$.,;:

abcdefghijklmnopqrstuvwxyz
ABCDEFGHIJKLMNOPQRSTUVWXYZ
1234567890 &?!£$.,;:

abcdefghijklmnopqrstuvwxyz
ABCDEFGHIJKLMNOPQRSTUVWXYZ
1234567890 &?!£$.,;:

abcdefghijklmnopqrstuvwxyz
ABCDEFGHIJKLMNOPQRSTUVWXYZ
1234567890 &?!£$.,;:

Breughel

Adrian Frutiger
Linotype (Stempel)
1981

Medium, medium italic, bold, bold italic, black, black italic

abcdefghijklmnopqrstuvwxyz
ABCDEFGHIJKLMNOPQRSTUVWXYZ
1234567890 1234567890 &£$.,:;!?"

abcdefghijklmnopqrstuvwxyz
ABCDEFGHIJKLMNOPQRSTUVWXYZ
1234567890 1234567890 &£$.,:;!?"

abcdefghijklmnopqrstuvwxyz
ABCDEFGHIJKLMNOPQRSTUVWXYZ
1234567890 1234567890 &£$.,:;!?"

abcdefghijklmnopqrstuvwxyz
ABCDEFGHIJKLMNOPQRSTUVWXYZ
1234567890 1234567890 &£$.,:;!?"

Brighton

Alan Bright
Letraset
1979

Compugraphic, Hell, Linotype, Scangraphic, Varityper

Light, light italic, medium, bold

Design conceived by Alan Bright and project completed primarily by Freda Sack in the Letraset studio

abcdefghijkklmnopqrstʃuvwxyz
ABCDEFGHIJKKLLMNOPQRRSTUVWXYZ
1234567890 &?!£$.,:;

abcdefghijkklmnopqrstʃuvwxyz
ABCDEFGHIJKKLLMNOPQRRSTUVWXYZ
1234567890 &?!£$.,:;

abcdefghijkklmnopqrstʃuvwxyz
ABCDEFGHIJKKLLMNOPQRRSTUVWXYZ
1234567890 &?!£$.,:;

abcdefghijkklmnopqrstʃuvwxyz
ABCDEFGHIJKKLLMNOPQRRSTUVWXYZ
1234567890 &?!£$.,:;

39

Bryn Mawr

Joseph Treacy
Linotype
1983

Light, light italic, book, book italic, medium, medium italic, bold, bold italic

abcdefghijklmnopqrstuvwxyz
ABCDEFGHIJKLMNOPQRSTUVWXYZ
1234567890 &£$.,:;!?"

abcdefghijklmnopqrstuvwxyz
ABCDEFGHIJKLMNOPQRSTUVWXYZ
1234567890 &£$.,:;!?"

abcdefghijklmnopqrstuvwxyz
ABCDEFGHIJKLMNOPQRSTUVWXYZ
1234567890 &£$.,:;!?"

abcdefghijklmnopqrstuvwxyz
ABCDEFGHIJKLMNOPQRSTUVWXYZ
1234567890 &£$.,:;!?"

Calisto

Ron Carpenter
Monotype
1987

Regular, regular italic, bold, bold italic

abcdefghijklmnopqrstuvwxyz
ABCDEFGHIJKLMNOPQRSTUVWXYZ
1234567890 .,:;!?"

abcdefghijklmnopqrstuvwxyz
ABCDEFGHIJKLMNOPQRSTUVWXYZ
1234567890 .,:;!?"

abcdefghijklmnopqrstuvwxyz
ABCDEFGHIJKLMNOPQRSTUVWXYZ
1234567890 .,:;!?"

abcdefghijklmnopqrstuvwxyz
ABCDEFGHIJKLMNOPQRSTUVWXYZ
1234567890 .,:;!?"

Calvert

Margaret Calvert
Monotype
1980

Light, medium, bold

Derived from lettering developed
for signs on the Tyne and Wear
Metro. Sloped roman versions are
intended to be extrapolated on a
digital phototypesetter

abcdefghijklmnopqrstuvwxyz
ABCDEFGHIJKLMNOPQRSTUVWXYZ
1234567890 .,:;!?''

abcdefghijklmnopqrstuvwxyz
ABCDEFGHIJKLMNOPQRSTUVWXYZ
1234567890 .,:;!?''

Campanile (previously Avanti)

Neville Brody
Linotype
1989

Roman

Designed for *Avanti* magazine
launched in 1986. Suitable only for
display composition

abcdefghijklmnopqrstuvwxyz
ABCDEFGHIJKLMNOPQRSTUVWXYZ
1234567890 &£$.,:;!?''

Cantoria

Ron Carpenter
Monotype
1986

Light, light italic, medium, medium
italic, semi bold, semi bold italic,
bold, bold italic, extra bold, extra
bold italic

Owes something to Della Robbia,
the design of Thomas Cleland
issued by Monotype in 1902

abcdefghijklmnopqrstuvwxyz
ABCDEFGHIJKLMNOPQRSTUVWXYZ
1234567890 .,:;!?''

abcdefghijklmnopqrstuvwxyz
ABCDEFGHIJKLMNOPQRSTUVWXYZ
1234567890 .,:;!?''

abcdefghijklmnopqrstuvwxyz
ABCDEFGHIJKLMNOPQRSTUVWXYZ
1234567890 .,:;!?''

abcdefghijklmnopqrstuvwxyz
ABCDEFGHIJKLMNOPQRSTUVWXYZ
1234567890 .,:;!?''

Bitstream Carmina

Gudrun Zapf-von Hesse
Bitstream
1987

Light, light italic, medium, medium italic, bold, bold italic, black, black italic

abcdefghijklmnopqrstuvwxyz
ABCDEFGHIJKLMNOPQRSTUVWXYZ
1234567890 &£$.,:;!?''

abcdefghijklmnopqrstuvwxyz
ABCDEFGHIJKLMNOPQRSTUVWXYZ
1234567890 &£$.,:;!?''

abcdefghijklmnopqrstuvwxyz
ABCDEFGHIJKLMNOPQRSTUVWXYZ
1234567890 &£$.,:;!?''

abcdefghijklmnopqrstuvwxyz
ABCDEFGHIJKLMNOPQRSTUVWXYZ
1234567890 &£$.,:;!?''

WTC Carnase Text

Tom Carnase
World Typeface Center
1982

Linotype

Light, light italic, regular, regular italic, medium, medium italic, bold, bold italic, extra bold, extra bold italic

First design issued by the World Typeface Center

abcdefghijklmnopqrstuvwxyz
ABCDEFGHIJKLMNOPQRSTUVWXYZ
1234567890 &£.,:;!?''

abcdefghijklmnopqrstuvwxyz
ABCDEFGHIJKLMNOPQRSTUVWXYZ
1234567890 &£.,:;!?''

abcdefghijklmnopqrstuvwxyz
ABCDEFGHIJKLMNOPQRSTUVWXYZ
1234567890 &£.,:;!?''

abcdefghijklmnopqrstuvwxyz
ABCDEFGHIJKLMNOPQRSTUVWXYZ
1234567890 &£.,:;!?''

Cartier

Carl Dair
Visual Graphics Corporation
1967

Compugraphic, Linotype, Varityper

Roman and italic

Designed specifically for phototypesetting and first used by Cape & Co, the Canadian printing house. One peculiarity is the lack of italic capitals. See Raleigh for details on further development of the style

abcdefghijklmnopqrstuvwxyz
ABCDEFGHIJKLMNOPQRSTUVWXYZ
1234567890 &£.,:;!?''

abcdefghijklmnopqrstuvwxyz
ABCDEFGHIJKLMNOPQRSTUVWXYZ
1234567890 &£.,:;!?''

Cascade Script

Matthew Carter
Linotype
1965

Kaskade Script (Autologic)
Freehand 471 (Bitstream)

One weight only

One of the first scripts developed by Linotype for phototypesetting

abcdefghijklmnopqrstuvwxyz
ABCDEFGHIJKLMNOPQRSTUVWXYZ
1234567890 &£$.,:;!?"

Caslon Buch

Günter Gerhard Lange
Berthold
1977

Regular, regular italic, medium, bold

abcdefghijklmnopqrstuvwxyz
ABCDEFGHIJKLMNOPQRSTUVWXYZ
1234567890 1234567890 &£$.,:;!?"

abcdefghijklmnopqrstuvwxyz
ABCDEFGHIJKLMNOPQRSTUVWXYZ
1234567890 &£$.,:;!?"

abcdefghijklmnopqrstuvwxyz
ABCDEFGHIJKLMNOPQRSTUVWXYZ
1234567890 &£$.,:;!?"

ITC Caslon 224

Edward Benguiat
International Typeface Corporation
1983

Autologic, Berthold, Compugraphic,
Linotype, Monotype, Scangraphic,
Varityper

Book, book italic, medium, medium
italic, bold, bold italic, black, black
italic

Freely adapted from the eighteenth-
century design by William Caslon

abcdefghijklmnopqrstuvwxyz
ABCDEFGHIJKLMNOPQRSTUVWXYZ
1234567890 &£$.,:;!?"

abcdefghijklmnopqrstuvwxyz
ABCDEFGHIJKLMNOPQRSTUVWXYZ
1234567890 &£$.,:;!?"

abcdefghijklmnopqrstuvwxyz
ABCDEFGHIJKLMNOPQRSTUVWXYZ
1234567890 &£$.,:;!?"

abcdefghijklmnopqrstuvwxyz
ABCDEFGHIJKLMNOPQRSTUVWXYZ
1234567890 &£$.,:;!?"

Catalana

Edward Benguiat
Compugraphic
1989

Book, book italic, bold, bold italic,
extra bold

Official typeface for the Olympic
Games of 1992 in Barcelona

Withdrawn

Catull

Gustav Jaeger
Berthold
1982

Regular, regular italic, medium, bold

abcdefghijklmnopqrstuvwxyz
ABCDEFGHIJKLMNOPQRSTUVWXYZ
1234567890 &£$.,:;!?''

abcdefghijklmnopqrstuvwxyz
ABCDEFGHIJKLMNOPQRSTUVWXYZ
1234567890 &£$.,:;!?''

abcdefghijklmnopqrstuvwxyz
ABCDEFGHIJKLMNOPQRSTUVWXYZ
1234567890 &£$.,:;!?''

Caxton

Leslie Usherwood
Letraset
1981

Compugraphic, Hell, Linotype,
Monotype, Scangraphic, Varityper
Calligraphic 816 (Bitstream)

Light, light italic, book, book italic,
bold, bold italic, extra bold, extra
bold italic, bold condensed, extra
bold condensed

Design prepared originally for
Typesettra Ltd in Toronto, a design
studio owned by the late Leslie
Usherwood (1932-82). Rights in the
typeface were assigned to Letraset
in 1981

abcdefghijklmnopqrstuvwxyz
ABCDEFGHIJKLMNOPQRSTUVWYZ
1234567890 &?!£$.,;:

abcdefghijklmnopqrstuvwxyz
ABCDEFGHIJKLMNOPQRSTUVWXYZ
1234567890 &?!£$.,;:

abcdefghijklmnopqrstuvwxyz
ABCDEFGHIJKLMNOPQRSTUVWXYZ
1234567890 &?!£$.,;:

abcdefghijklmnopqrstuvwxyz
ABCDEFGHIJKLMNOPQRSTUVWXYZ
1234567890 &?!£$.,;:

Linotype Centennial

Adrian Frutiger
Linotype
1986

Adobe

Light, light italic, regular, regular italic, bold, bold italic, black, black italic

Issued in the centenary year of the Linotype Group of Companies celebrating the invention during 1886 of the Blower Linotype hot-metal machine by Ottmar Mergenthaler

abcdefghijklmnopqrstuvwxyz
ABCDEFGHIJKLMNOPQRSTUVWXYZ
1234567890 1234567890 &£$.,:;!?"

abcdefghijklmnopqrstuvwxyz
ABCDEFGHIJKLMNOPQRSTUVWXYZ
1234567890 1234567890 &£$.,:;!?"

abcdefghijklmnopqrstuvwxyz
ABCDEFGHIJKLMNOPQRSTUVWXYZ
1234567890 1234567890 &£$.,:;!?"

abcdefghijklmnopqrstuvwxyz
ABCDEFGHIJKLMNOPQRSTUVWXYZ
1234567890 1234567890 &£$.,:;!?"

ITC Century

Tony Stan
International Typeface Corporation
1975

Autologic, Berthold, Compugraphic, Hell, Linotype, Monotype, Scangraphic, Varityper
Century 711 (Bitstream)

Light, light italic, book, book italic, bold, bold italic, ultra, ultra italic, light condensed, light condensed italic, book condensed, book condensed italic, bold condensed, bold condensed italic, ultra condensed, ultra condensed italic

Issued under licence from the American Type Founders Co. Ultra and book weights, with complementary italics, were released by ITC in 1975; the rest of the family ensued in 1980. The original ATF Century was designed by Theodore L De Vinne for *The Century* magazine in 1895 and was developed into eighteen variants by Morris Fuller Benton between 1900 and 1928

abcdefghijklmnopqrstuvwxyz
ABCDEFGHIJKLMNOPQRSTUVWXYZ
1234567890 &£$.,:;!?"

abcdefghijklmnopqrstuvwxyz
ABCDEFGHIJKLMNOPQRSTUVWXYZ
1234567890 &£$.,:;!?"

abcdefghijklmnopqrstuvwxyz
ABCDEFGHIJKLMNOPQRSTUVWXYZ
1234567890 &£$.,:;!?"

abcdefghijklmnopqrstuvwxyz
ABCDEFGHIJKLMNOPQRSTUVWXYZ
1234567890 &£$.,:;!?"

Certificate Face Bold

Rick Lawrie
Itek
1982

One weight only

abcdefghijklmnopqrstuvwxyz
ABCDEFGHIJKLMNOPQRSTUVWXYZ
1234567890 &£$.,:;!?""

Champfleury

Staff designers
Autologic
1985

Titling, initials (outline, cameo, and normal), constructed initials (outline, cameo and normal)

Based on lettering by Geoffroy Tory, the French scholar of the sixteenth century

ABCDEFGHIJKLMNOP
QRSTUVWXYZ

Adobe Charlemagne

Carol Twombly
Adobe
1989

Regular, bold

ABCDEFGHIJKLMNOPQRSTUVWXYZ
1234567890 &£$.,:;!?"

ABCDEFGHIJKLMNOPQRSTUVWXYZ
1234567890 &£$.,:;!?"

Bitstream Charter

Matthew Carter
Bitstream
1987

Regular, regular italic, bold, bold italic, black, black italic

First original type design issued by Bitstream

abcdefghijklmnopqrstuvwxyz
ABCDEFGHIJKLMNOPQRSTUVWXYZ
1234567890 1234567890 &£$.,:;!?"

abcdefghijklmnopqrstuvwxyz
ABCDEFGHIJKLMNOPQRSTUVWXYZ
1234567890 1234567890 &£$.,:;!?"

abcdefghijklmnopqrstuvwxyz
ABCDEFGHIJKLMNOPQRSTUVWXYZ
1234567890 1234567890 &£$.,:;!?"

abcdefghijklmnopqrstuvwxyz
ABCDEFGHIJKLMNOPQRSTUVWXYZ
1234567890 1234567890 &£$.,:;!?"

Chasseur

Gustav Jaeger
Berthold
1988

Light, light italic, regular, regular italic, medium, medium italic, bold, bold italic

abcdefghijklmnopqrstuvwxyz
ABCDEFGHIJKLMNOPQRSTUVWXYZ
1234567890 &£$.,:;!?"

abcdefghijklmnopqrstuvwxyz
ABCDEFGHIJKLMNOPQRSTUVWXYZ
1234567890 &£$.,:;!?"

abcdefghijklmnopqrstuvwxyz
ABCDEFGHIJKLMNOPQRSTUVWXYZ
1234567890 &£$.,:;!?"

abcdefghijklmnopqrstuvwxyz
ABCDEFGHIJKLMNOPQRSTUVWXYZ
1234567890 &£$.,:;!?"

ITC Cheltenham

Tony Stan
International Typeface Corporation
1975

Adobe, Autologic, Berthold,
Compugraphic, Hell, Linotype,
Monotype, Scangraphic, Varityper
Stubserif 705 (Bitstream)
CH (Itek)

Light, light italic, book, book italic,
bold, bold italic, ultra, ultra italic,
light condensed, light condensed
italic, book condensed, book
condensed italic, bold condensed,
bold condensed italic, ultra
condensed, ultra condensed italic

Ultra and book weights were issued
by ITC in 1975 followed by the rest
of the family in 1978. The original
Cheltenham typeface was cut by the
American Type Founders Co in 1896
after the design of Bertram
Goodhue, an architect. It was
restricted initially to the use of the
Cheltenham Press run by Ingalls
Kimball in New York. Both ATF and
Linotype collaborated to release the
typeface to the general printing
trade between 1904 and 1911 and
expanded the family to eighteen
variants

abcdefghijklmnopqrstuvwxyz
ABCDEFGHIJKLMNOPQRSTUVWXYZ
1234567890 &£$.,:;!?"

abcdefghijklmnopqrstuvwxyz
ABCDEFGHIJKLMNOPQRSTUVWXYZ
1234567890 &£$.,:;!?"

abcdefghijklmnopqrstuvwxyz
ABCDEFGHIJKLMNOPQRSTUVWXYZ
1234567890 &£$.,:;!?"

abcdefghijklmnopqrstuvwxyz
ABCDEFGHIJKLMNOPQRSTUVWXYZ
1234567890 &£$.,:;!?"

Churchward 69

Joseph Churchward
Churchward International
1969

Berthold

Elongated, elongated italic, bold
condensed, bold condensed italic,
extra bold, extra bold italic, ultra
bold, ultra bold italic

Churchward 69
Churchward 69
Churchward 69
Churchward 69

Churchward 70

Joseph Churchward
Churchward International
1970

Berthold, Linotype

Hairline, hairline italic, light, light
italic, regular, medium, medium
italic, demi bold, demi bold italic,
bold, bold italic, ultra bold, ultra
bold italic, chisel, deep shadow
regular, deep shadow regular italic,
double, lines, lines deep shadow
regular, lines deep shadow regular
italic, metallic, modern regular,
modern regular italic, no-end,
sparkly regular, sparkly regular
italic

abcdefghijklmnopqrstuvwxyz
ABCDEFGHIJKLMNOPQRSTUVWXYZ
1234567890 &£ſ.,:;!?"

abcdefghijklmnopqrstuvwxyz
ABCDEFGHIJKLMNOPQRSTUVWXYZ
1234567890 &£ſ.,:;!?"

Claridge

Adrian Williams
Fonts/Ingrama SA
1979

Compugraphic

Regular, regular italic, bold, black

abcdefghijklmnopqrstuvwxyz
ABCDEFGH̃IJKLMNOPQRSTUVWXYZ
1234567890 (.,:;''*¿?¡!)%¢$/&

abcdefghijklmnopqrstuvwxyz
ABCDEFGH̃IJKLMNOPQRSTUVWXYZ
1234567890 (.,:;''¿?¡!)%¢$/ &*

abcdefghijklmnopqrstuvwxyz
ABCDEFGH̃IJKLMNOPQRSTUVWXYZ
1234567890 (.,:;''*¿?¡!)%¢$/&

abcdefghijklmnopqrstuvwxyz
ABCDEFGH̃IJKLMNOPQRSTUVWXYZ
1234567890 (.,:;''*¿?¡!)%¢$/&

Clarion

Staff designers
Monotype
1983

Regular, regular italic, bold

abcdefghijklmnopqrstuvwxyz
ABCDEFGHIJKLMNOPQRSTUVWXYZ
1234567890 .,:;!?''

abcdefghijklmnopqrstuvwxyz
ABCDEFGHIJKLMNOPQRSTUVWXYZ
1234567890 .,:;!?''

abcdefghijklmnopqrstuvwxyz
ABCDEFGHIJKLMNOPQRSTUVWXYZ
1234567890 .,:;!?''

ITC Clearface

Victor Caruso
International Typeface Corporation
1979

Adobe, Autologic, Berthold,
Compugraphic, Linotype,
Monotype, Scangraphic, Varityper
Revival 814 (Bitstream)
CF (Itek)

Regular, regular italic, bold, bold
italic, heavy, heavy italic, black,
black italic

Based on the design Clearface by
Morris Fuller Benton for the
American Type Founders Co in 1907

abcdefghijklmnopqrstuvwxyz
ABCDEFGHIJKLMNOPQRSTUVWXYZ
1234567890 &£$.,:;!?"

abcdefghijklmnopqrstuvwxyz
ABCDEFGHIJKLMNOPQRSTUVWXYZ
1234567890 &£$.,:;!?"

abcdefghijklmnopqrstuvwxyz
ABCDEFGHIJKLMNOPQRSTUVWXYZ
1234567890 &£$.,:;!?"

abcdefghijklmnopqrstuvwxyz
ABCDEFGHIJKLMNOPQRSTUVWXYZ
1234567890 &£$.,:;!?"

Cloe

Linda Hoffman
Varityper
1979

One weight only

abcdefghijklmnopqrstuvwxyz
ABCDEFGHIJKLMNOPQRSTUVWXYZ
1234567890 &£$.,:;!?"

abcdefghijklmnopqrstuvwxyz
ABCDEFGHIJKLMNOPQRSTUVWXYZ
1234567890 &£$.,:;!?"

Cochin

Matthew Carter
Linotype (Mergenthaler)
1977

Adobe
CG Collage (Compugraphic)
Traverse (Varityper)

Regular, regular italic, bold, bold italic, black, black italic

Re-working of an eighteenth-century French design. Most type sources include a Cochin design in their libraries

abcdefghijklmnopqrstuvwxyz
ABCDEFGHIJKLMNOPQRSTUVWXYZ
1234567890 &£$.,:;!?''

abcdefghijklmnopqrstuvwxyz
ABCDEFGHIJKLMNOPQRSTUVWXYZ
1234567890 &£$.,:;!?''

abcdefghijklmnopqrstuvwxyz
ABCDEFGHIJKLMNOPQRSTUVWXYZ
1234567890 &£$.,:;!?''

abcdefghijklmnopqrstuvwxyz
ABCDEFGHIJKLMNOPQRSTUVWXYZ
1234567890 &£$.,:;!?''

Colossal

Aldo Novarese
Berthold
1984

Regular, medium, bold, black

abcdefghijklmnopqrstuvwxyz
ABCDEFGHIJKLMNOPQRSTUVWXYZ
1234567890 &£$.,:;!?''

abcdefghijklmnopqrstuvwxyz
ABCDEFGHIJKLMNOPQRSTUVWXYZ
1234567890 &£$.,:;!?''

Comenius

Hermann Zapf
Berthold
1976

Regular, regular italic, medium, bold

Type named after Jan Amos Comenius (1592-1670), who published *Orbis Sensualum Pictus* (The Visible World) in 1659. It was the first textbook to contain illustrations specially for children

abcdefghijklmnopqrstuvwxyz
ABCDEFGHIJKLMNOPQRSTUVWXYZ
1234567890 &£$.,:;!?"

abcdefghijklmnopqrstuvwxyz
ABCDEFGHIJKLMNOPQRSTUVWXYZ
1234567890 &£$.,:;!?"

abcdefghijklmnopqrstuvwxyz
ABCDEFGHIJKLMNOPQRSTUVWXYZ
1234567890 &£$.,:;!?"

Compacta

Frederick Lambert
Letraset
1963

Autologic, Berthold, Hell, Linotype, Scangraphic, Varityper
Swiss 930 (Bitstream)

Light, regular, regular italic, bold, bold italic, black

abcdefghijklmnopqrstuvwxyz
ABCDEFGHIJKLMNOPQRSTUVWXYZ
1234567890 &?!€$.,;:

abcdefghijklmnopqrstuvwxyz
ABCDEFGHIJKLMNOPQRSTUVWXYZ
1234567890 &?!€$.,;:

abcdefghijklmnopqrstuvwxyz
ABCDEFGHIJKLMNOPQRSTUVWXYZ
1234567890 &?!€$.,;:

abcdefghijklmnopqrstuvwxyz
ABCDEFGHIJKLMNOPQRSTUVWXYZ
1234567890 &?!€$.,;:

Compus

Ferdinay Duman
Hell
1989

Regular, outline, shadow

abcdefghijklmnopqrstuvwxyz
ABCDEFGHIJKLMNOPQRSTUVWXYZ
1234567890 &£$.,:;!?"

abcdefghijklmnopqrstuvwxyz
ABCDEFGHIJKLMNOPQRSTUVWXYZ
1234567890 &£$.,:;!?"

abcdefghijklmnopqrstuvwxyz
ABCDEFGHIJKLMNOPQRSTUVWXYZ
1234567890 &£$.,:;!?"

Concorde

Günter Gerhard Lange
Berthold
1969

Linotype, Monotype
CJ (Itek)
Chinchilla (Scangraphic)
Transport (Varityper)

Regular, regular italic, regular condensed, medium, medium italic, medium condensed, bold condensed, bold condensed outline

abcdefghijklmnopqrstuvwxyz
ABCDEFGHIJKLMNOPQRSTUVWXYZ
1234567890 1234567890 &£$.,:;!?"

abcdefghijklmnopqrstuvwxyz
ABCDEFGHIJKLMNOPQRSTUVWXYZ
1234567890 &£$.,:;!?"

abcdefghijklmnopqrstuvwxyz
ABCDEFGHIJKLMNOPQRSTUVWXYZ
1234567890 &£$.,:;!?"

abcdefghijklmnopqrstuvwxyz
ABCDEFGHIJKLMNOPQRSTUVWXYZ
1234567890 &£$.,:;!?"

Concorde Nova

Günter Gerhard Lange
Berthold
1975

Regular, regular italic, medium

abcdefghijklmnopqrstuvwxyz
ABCDEFGHIJKLMNOPQRSTUVWXYZ
1234567890 &£$.,:;!?"

abcdefghijklmnopqrstuvwxyz
ABCDEFGHIJKLMNOPQRSTUVWXYZ
1234567890 &£$.,:;!?"

abcdefghijklmnopqrstuvwxyz
ABCDEFGHIJKLMNOPQRSTUVWXYZ
1234567890 &£$.,:;!?"

Congress

Adrian Williams
Fonts/Ingrama SA
1980

Autologic, Compugraphic, Linotype, Scangraphic

Light, regular, regular italic, medium, bold, heavy, cameo

Released at Basle in 1980 to coincide with the Congress of the Association Typographique Internationale (ATypI)

abcdefghijklmnopqrstuvwxyz
ABCDEFGHIJKLMNOPQRSTUVWXYZ
1234567890 &£$.,:;!?''

abcdefghijklmnopqrstuvwxyz
ABCDEFGHIJKLMNOPQRSTUVWXYZ
1234567890 &£$.,:;!?''

abcdefghijklmnopqrstuvwxyz
ABCDEFGHIJKLMNOPQRSTUVWXYZ
1234567890 &£$.,:;!?''

Contempo

Vladimir Andrich
Alphatype
1967

Regular, bold

abcdefghijklmnopqrstuvwxyz
ABCDEFGHIJKLMNOPQRSTUVWXYZ
1234567890 &£$.,:;!?"

abcdefghijklmnopqrstuvwxyz
ABCDEFGHIJKLMNOPQRSTUVWXYZ
1234567890 &£$.,:;!?"

Contura

Dick Dooijes
Lettergietterij Amsterdam
1966

Berthold

One weight only of roman

abcdefghijklmnopqpqrstuvwxyz
ABCDEFGHIJKLMNOPQRSTUVWXYZ
1234567890 &£$.,:;!?"

Bitstream Cooper

Staff designers
Bitstream
1986

Light, light italic, medium, medium
italic, bold, bold italic

Extended family derived from
Cooper Black designed by Oswald
Cooper for the typefoundry
Barnhard Brothers & Spindler in
1921

abcdefghijklmnopqrstuvwxyz
ABCDEFGHIJKLMNOPQRSTUVWXYZ
1234567890 &£$.,:;!?''

abcdefghijklmnopqrstuvwxyz
ABCDEFGHIJKLMNOPQRSTUVWXYZ
1234567890 &£$.,:;!?''

abcdefghijklmnopqrstuvwxyz
ABCDEFGHIJKLMNOPQRSTUVWXYZ
1234567890 &£$.,:;!?"

abcdefghijklmnopqrstuvwxyz
ABCDEFGHIJKLMNOPQRSTUVWXYZ
1234567890 &£$.,:;!?"

Corinthian

Colin Brignall
Letraset
1981

Varityper

Light, medium, bold, bold
condensed, extra bold

Designer was influenced by the type
of Edward Johnston for London
Transport

abcdefghijklmnopqrstuvwxyz
ABCDEFGHIJKLMNOPQRSTUVWXYZ
1234567890 &?!£$.,;:

abcdefghijklmnopqrstuvwxyz
ABCDEFGHIJKLMNOPQRSTUVWXYZ
1234567890 &?!£$.,;:

abcdefghijklmnopqrstuvwxyz
ABCDEFGHIJKLMNOPQRSTUVWXYZ
1234567890 &?!£$.,;:

abcdefghijklmnopqrstuvwxyz
ABCDEFGHIJKLMNOPQRSTUVWXYZ
1234567890 &?!£$.,;:

Cosmos

Gustav Jaeger
Berthold
1982

Light, light italic, medium, extra
bold

abcdefghijklmnopqrstuvwxyz
ABCDEFGHIJKLMNOPQRSTUVWXYZ
1234567890 &£$.,:;!?"

abcdefghijklmnopqrstuvwxyz
ABCDEFGHIJKLMNOPQRSTUVWXYZ
1234567890

abcdefghijklmnopqrstuvwxyz
ABCDEFGHIJKLMNOPQRSTUVWXYZ
1234567890 &£$.,:;!?"

For **Cornet** see Supplement

57

Adobe Cottonwood

Anonymous
Adobe
1990

One weight only

Based on an early American design
for wood letter

ABCDEFGHIJKLMNOPQRSTUVWXYZ
1234567890 &£$.,:;!?"

Cremona

Vladimir Andrich
Alphatype
1982

Berthold

Regular, regular italic, bold, bold
italic

abcdefghijklmnopqrstuvwxyz
ABCDEFGHIJKLMNOPQRSTUVWXYZ
1234567890 1234567890 &£$.,:;!?"

abcdefghijklmnopqrstuvwxyz
ABCDEFGHIJKLMNOPQRSTUVWXYZ
1234567890 &£$.,:;!?"

abcdefghijklmnopqrstuvwxyz
ABCDEFGHIJKLMNOPQRSTUVWXYZ
1234567890 &£$.,:;!?"

abcdefghijklmnopqrstuvwxyz
ABCDEFGHIJKLMNOPQRSTUVWXYZ
1234567890 &£$.,:;!?"

Crillee

Dick Jones
Letraset
1980

Hell, Linotype, Scangraphic, Varityper

Light italic, regular italic, bold italic, extra bold italic

abcdefghijklmnopqrstuvwxyz
ABCDEFGHIJKLMNOPQRSTUVWXYZ
1234567890 &?!£$.,;:

abcdefghijklmnopqrstuvwxyz
ABCDEFGHIJKLMNOPQRSTUVWXYZ
1234567890 &?!£$.,;.

abcdefghijklmnopqrstuvwxyz
ABCDEFGHIJKLMNOPQRSTUVWXYZ
1234567890 &?!£$.,;:

abcdefghijklmnopqrstuvwxyz
ABCDEFGHIJKLMNOPQRSTUVWXYZ
1234567890 &?!£$.,;:

Criterion

Phil Martin
TypeSpectra
1982

Autologic, Compugraphic, Linotype

Light, light italic, book, book italic, medium, bold

abcdefghijklmnopqrstuvwxyz
ABCDEFGHIJKLMNOPQRSTUVWXYZ
1234567890 &£.,:;!?"

abcdefghijklmnopqrstuvwxyz
ABCDEFGHIJKLMNOPQRSTUVWXYZ
1234567890 &£.,:;!?"

abcdefghijklmnopqrstuvwxyz
ABCDEFGHIJKLMNOPQRSTUVWXYZ
1234567890 &£.,:;!?"

abcdefghijklmnopqrstuvwxyz
ABCDEFGHIJKLMNOPQRSTUVWXYZ
1234567890 &£.,:;!?"

WTC Cursivium

Jelle Bosma
World Typeface Center
1986

Linotype

Light, light italic, regular, regular italic, medium, medium italic, bold, bold italic

Sixth design issued by the World Typeface Center

abcdefghijklmnopqrstuvwxyz
ABCDEFGHIJKLMNOPQRSTUVWXYZ
1234567890 &£.,:;!?''

abcdefghijklmnopqrstuvwxyz
ABCDEFGHIJKLMNOPQRSTUVWXYZ
1234567890 &£.,:;!?''

abcdefghijklmnopqrstuvwxyz
ABCDEFGHIJKLMNOPQRSTUVWXYZ
1234567890 &£.,:;!?''

abcdefghijklmnopqrstuvwxyz
ABCDEFGHIJKLMNOPQRSTUVWXYZ
1234567890 &£.,:;!?''

ITC Cushing

Vincent Pacella
International Typeface Corporation
1982

Autologic, Berthold, Compugraphic, Linotype, Scangraphic, Varityper
Revival 721 (Bitstream)

Book, book italic, medium, medium italic, bold, bold italic, heavy, heavy italic

Based on Lining Cushing Old Style No.2 released by the American Type Founders Co. between 1897 and 1904. J Stearns designed the roman at the earlier date and Frederic W Goudy the italic at the later date

abcdefghijklmnopqrstuvwxyz
ABCDEFGHIJKLMNOPQRSTUVWXYZ
1234567890 &£$.,:;!?''

abcdefghijklmnopqrstuvwxyz
ABCDEFGHIJKLMNOPQRSTUVWXYZ
1234567890 &£$.,:;!?''

abcdefghijklmnopqrstuvwxyz
ABCDEFGHIJKLMNOPQRSTUVWXYZ
1234567890 &£$.,:;!?''

abcdefghijklmnopqrstuvwxyz
ABCDEFGHIJKLMNOPQRSTUVWXYZ
1234567890 &£$.,:;!?''

Cyrano

Gerard Unger
Hell
1989

Light, light italic, bold, bold italic

abcdefghijklmnopqrstuvwxyz
ABCDEFGHIJKLMNOPQRSTUVWXYZ
1234567890 &£$.,:;!?''

**abcdefghijklmnopqrstuvwxyz
ABCDEFGHIJKLMNOPQRSTUVWXYZ
1234567890 &£$.,:;!?''**

*abcdefghijklmnopqrstuvwxyz
ABCDEFGHIJKLMNOPQRSTUVWXYZ
1234567890 &£$.,:;!?''*

***abcdefghijklmnopqrstuvwxyz
ABCDEFGHIJKLMNOPQRSTUVWXYZ
1234567890 &£$.,:;!?''***

Daily News

Gustav Jaeger
Berthold
1985

Regular, regular italic, medium,
medium italic, bold, bold italic, extra
bold, extra bold italic

abcdefghijklmnopqrstuvwxyz
ABCDEFGHIJKLMNOPQRSTUVWXYZ
1234567890 &£$.,:;!?''

*abcdefghijklmnopqrstuvwxyz
ABCDEFGHIJKLMNOPQRSTUVWXYZ
1234567890 &£$.,:;!?''*

**abcdefghijklmnopqrstuvwxyz
ABCDEFGHIJKLMNOPQRSTUVWXYZ
1234567890 &£$.,:;!?''**

***abcdefghijklmnopqrstuvwxyz
ABCDEFGHIJKLMNOPQRSTUVWXYZ
1234567890 &£$.,:;!?''***

Dalcora

Erwin Koch
Hell
1989

Bold and outline

abcdefghijklmnopqrstuvwxyz
ABCDEFGHIJKLMNOPQRSTUVWXYZ
1234567890 &£$.,:;!?"'

abcdefghijklmnopqrstuvwxyz
ABCDEFGHIJKLMNOPQRSTUVWXYZ
1234567890 &£$.,:;!?"'

Delta

Gustav Jaeger
Berthold
1983

Light, light italic, book, book italic,
medium, medium italic, bold, bold
italic, outline

abcdefghijklmnopqrstuvwxyz
ABCDEFGHIJKLMNOPQRSTUVWXYZ
1234567890 &£$.,:;!?"

abcdefghijklmnopqrstuvwxyz
ABCDEFGHIJKLMNOPQRSTUVWXYZ
1234567890 &£$.,:;!?"

abcdefghijklmnopqrstuvwxyz
ABCDEFGHIJKLMNOPQRSTUVWXYZ
1234567890 &£$.,:;!?"

abcdefghijklmnopqrstuvwxyz
ABCDEFGHIJKLMNOPQRSTUVWXYZ
1234567890 &£$.,:;!?"

Demos

Gerard Unger
Hell
1976

Scangraphic

Medium, medium italic, semi bold

Serif roman complement to Praxis
(q.v.)

abcdefghijklmnopqrstuvwxyz
ABCDEFGHIJKLMNOPQRSTUVWXYZ
1234567890 1234567890 &£$.,:;!?"

abcdefghijklmnopqrstuvwxyz
ABCDEFGHIJKLMNOPQRSTUVWXYZ
1234567890 1234567890 &£$.,:;!?"

abcdefghijklmnopqrstuvwxyz
ABCDEFGHIJKLMNOPQRSTUVWXYZ
1234567890 1234567890 &£$.,:;!?"

Devendra

D Thaker
Linotype (Mergenthaler)
1982

One weight only

abcdefghijklmnopqrstuvwxyz
ABCDEFGHIJKLMNOPQRSTUVWXYZ
1234567890 &£$.,:;!?"

Digi-Grotesk Series S

Staff designers
Hell
1968

Berthold

Light, semi bold

One of the earliest typefaces to be
designed specially for digital CRT
phototypesetting

abcdefghijklmnopqrstuvwxyz
ABCDEFGHIJKLMNOPQRSTUVWXYZ
1234567890 &£$.,!?"

abcdefghijklmnopqrstuvwxyz
ABCDEFGHIJKLMNOPQRSTUVWXYZ
1234567890 &£$.,!?"

Draco

Joffre Lefevre
Compugraphic
1984

Light, medium, bold

Part of the Novus collection with
Pictor and Vela and designed to
complement electronic modulation
of the letter forms

abcdefghijklmnopqrstuvwxyz
ABCDEFGHIJKLMNOPQRSTUVWXYZ
1234567890(.,:;"?!)$%/&

abcdefghijklmnopqrstuvwxyz
ABCDEFGHIJKLMNOPQRSTUVWXYZ
1234567890(.,:;"?!)$%/&

abcdefghijklmnopqrstuvwxyz
ABCDEFGHIJKLMNOPQRSTUVWXYZ
1234567890(.,:;"?!)$%/&

Edison

Hermann Zapf
Hell
1977

Scangraphic

Book, book italic, semi bold, semi
bold italic, bold

Intended primarily for newspaper
and technical texts. Cyrillic styles
are available to complement the
Latin alphabets

abcdefghijklmnopqrstuvwxyz
ABCDEFGHIJKLMNOPQRSTUVWXYZ
1234567890 &£$.,:;!?''

abcdefghijklmnopqrstuvwxyz
ABCDEFGHIJKLMNOPQRSTUVWXYZ
1234567890 &£$.,:;!?''

abcdefghijklmnopqrstuvwxyz
ABCDEFGHIJKLMNOPQRSTUVWXYZ
1234567890 &£$.,:;!?''

abcdefghijklmnopqrstuvwxyz
ABCDEFGHIJKLMNOPQRSTUVWXYZ
1234567890 &£$.,:;!?''

Edwardian

Colin Brignall
Letraset
1983

Varityper

Light, light italic, medium, medium italic, bold, bold italic, extra bold, extra bold italic

abcdefghijklmnopqrstuvwxyz
ABCDEFGHIJKLMNOPQRSTUVWXYZ
1234567890 &?!£$.,;:

abcdefghijkllmnopqqurstuvwxyz
ABCDEFGHIJKLMNOPQRSTUVWXYZ
1234567890 &?!£$.,;:

abcdefghijklmnopqrstuvwxyz
ABCDEFGHIJKLMNOPQRSTUVWXYZ
1234567890 &?!£$.,;:

abcdefghijklmnopqrstuvwxyz
ABCDEFGHIJKLMNOPQRSTUVWXYZ
1234567890 &?!£$.,;:

Egyptian 505

André Gürtler
Visual Graphics Corporation
1966

Compugraphic, Linotype, Scangraphic
Egyptios (Autologic)
Egypt 55 (Varityper)

Light, regular, medium, bold

abcdefghijklmnopqrstuvwxyz
ABCDEFGHIJKLMNOPQRSTUVWXYZ
1234567890 &£.,:;!?''

abcdefghijklmnopqrstuvwxyz
ABCDEFGHIJKLMNOPQRSTUVWXYZ
1234567890 &£.,:;!?''

abcdefghijklmnopqrstuvwxyz
ABCDEFGHIJKLMNOPQRSTUVWXYZ
1234567890 &£.,:;!?''

abcdefghijklmnopqrstuvwxyz
ABCDEFGHIJKLMNOPQRSTUVWXYZ
1234567890 &£.,:;!?''

ITC Elan

Albert Boton
International Typeface Corporation
1985

Autologic, Berthold, Compugraphic,
Linotype, Scangraphic, Varityper
EI (Itek)

Book, book italic, medium, medium
italic, bold, bold italic, black, black
italic

Second typeface by Albert Boton for
ITC; the first was ITC Eras in 1976,
the result of collaboration with
Albert Hollenstein

abcdefghijklmnopqrstuvwxyz
ABCDEFGHIJKLMNOPQRSTUVWXYZ
1234567890 1234567890 &£$.,:;!?"

abcdefghijklmnopqrstuvwxyz
ABCDEFGHIJKLMNOPQRSTUVWXYZ
1234567890 1234567890 &£$.,:;!?"

abcdefghijklmnopqrstuvwxyz
ABCDEFGHIJKLMNOPQRSTUVWXYZ
1234567890 1234567890 &£$.,:;!?"

abcdefghijklmnopqrstuvwxyz
ABCDEFGHIJKLMNOPQRSTUVWXYZ
1234567890 1234567890 &£$.,:;!?"

El Greco

Günter Gerhard Lange
Berthold
1964

One weight only

abcdefghijklmnopqrstuvwxyz
ABCDEFGHIJKLMNOPQRSTUVWXYZ
1234567890 &£$.,!?"

Ellington

Michael Harvey
Monotype
1990

Light, light italic, roman, italic, bold, bold italic, extra bold, extra bold italic

Named after the jazz musician Duke Ellington

abcdefghijklmnopqrstuvwxyz
ABCDEFGHIJKLMNOPQRSTUVWXYZ
1234567890 1234567890 &£$.,:;!''

abcdefghijklmnopqrstuvwxyz
ABCDEFGHIJKLMNOPQRSTUVWXYZ
1234567890 1234567890 &£$.,:;!''

abcdefghijklmnopqrstuvwxyz
ABCDEFGHIJKLMNOPQRSTUVWXYZ
1234567890 1234567890 &£$.,:;!''

abcdefghijklmnopqrstuvwxyz
ABCDEFGHIJKLMNOPQRSTUVWXYZ
1234567890 1234567890 &£$.,:;!''

Else

Robert Norton
Norton Photosetting
1982

Autologic, Linotype
EE (Itek)

Light, light italic, medium, medium italic, semi bold, semi bold italic, bold, bold italic

Greek and Cyrillic founts are available to work harmoniously with the Latin alphabets

abcdefghijklmnopqrstuvwxyz
ABCDEFGHIJKLMNOPQRSTUVWXYZ
1234567890 &£.,:;!?''

abcdefghijklmnopqrstuvwxyz
ABCDEFGHIJKLMNOPQRSTUVWXYZ
1234567890 &£.,:;!?''

abcdefghijklmnopqrstuvwxyz
ABCDEFGHIJKLMNOPQRSTUVWXYZ
1234567890 &£.,:;!?''

abcdefghijklmnopqrstuvwxyz
ABCDEFGHIJKLMNOPQRSTUVWXYZ
1234567890 &£.,:;!?''

Englische Schreibschrift

Staff designers
Berthold
1972

Scangraphic
English Script (Autologic)
English Script (Varityper)

Regular, medium, bold

abcdefghijklmnopqrstuvwxyz
ABCDEFGHIJKLMNOPQRSTUVWXYZ
1234567890 &£$.,:;!?''

abcdefghijklmnopqrstuvwxyz
ABCDEFGHIJKLMNOPQRSTUVWXYZ
1234567890 &£$.,:;!?''

Epikur

Gustav Jaeger
Berthold
1986

Light, light italic, regular, regular
italic, medium, medium italic, bold,
bold italic

abcdefghijklmnopqrstuvwxyz
ABCDEFGHIJKLMNOPQRSTUVWXYZ
1234567890 1234567890 &£$.,:;!?"

abcdefghijklmnopqrstuvwxyz
ABCDEFGHIJKLMNOPQRSTUVWXYZ
1234567890 &£$.,:;!?"

abcdefghijklmnopqrstuvwxyz
ABCDEFGHIJKLMNOPQRSTUVWXYZ
1234567890 &£$.,:;!?"

abcdefghijklmnopqrstuvwxyz
ABCDEFGHIJKLMNOPQRSTUVWXYZ
1234567890 &£$.,:;!?"

ITC Eras

Albert Boton and Albert Hollenstein
International Typeface Corporation
1976

Adobe, Autologic, Berthold,
Compugraphic, Hell, Linotype,
Monotype, Scangraphic, Varityper
Incised 726 (Bitstream)
ER (Itek)

Light, book, medium, demi, bold,
ultra, contour, outline

Originally designed for Studio
Hollenstein in Paris during 1969 and
cut by the Wagner typefoundry

abcdefghijklmnopqrstuvwxyz
ABCDEFGHIJKLMNOPQRSTUVWXYZ
1234567890 &£$.,:;!?"

abcdefghijklmnopqrstuvwxyz
ABCDEFGHIJKLMNOPQRSTUVWXYZ
1234567890 &£$.,:;!?"

ITC Esprit

Jovica Veljovic
International Typeface Corporation
1985

Autologic, Berthold, Compugraphic,
Linotype, Scangraphic, Varityper
EP (Itek)

Book, book italic, medium, medium
italic, bold, bold italic, black, black
italic

Second typeface by Jovica Veljovic
for ITC

abcdefghijklmnopqrstuvwxyz
ABCDEFGHIJKLMNOPQRSTUVWXYZ
1234567890 1234567890 &£$.,:;!?"

abcdefghijklmnopqrstuvwxyz
ABCDEFGHIJKLMNOPQRSTUVWXYZ
1234567890 1234567890 &£$.,:;!?"

abcdefghijklmnopqrstuvwxyz
ABCDEFGHIJKLMNOPQRSTUVWXYZ
1234567890 1234567890 &£$.,:;!?"

abcdefghijklmnopqrstuvwxyz
ABCDEFGHIJKLMNOPQRSTUVWXYZ
1234567890 1234567890 &£$.,:;!?"

Eurostile

Aldo Novarese
Nebiolo
1962

Adobe, Berthold, Linotype,
Monotype, Scangraphic, Varityper
Aldostyle (Autologic)
Square 721 (Bitstream)
Microstyle (Compugraphic)
ES (Itek)

Regular, regular italic, regular
condensed, regular extended, bold,
bold condensed, bold extended

Similar to the titling founts
Microgramma from the same
designer and founder, but offering
lower-case alphabets

abcdefghijklmnopqrstuvwxyz
ABCDEFGHIJKLMNOPQRSTUVWXYZ
1234567890 &£$.,:;!?"

abcdefghijklmnopqrstuvwxyz
ABCDEFGHIJKLMNOPQRSTUVWXYZ
1234567890 &£$.,:;!?"

Expert

Aldo Novarese
Haas
1983

Linotype

Light, light italic, regular, regular italic, bold, black

Prompted by Renaissance, a typeface in the Haas typefoundry collection

abcdefghijklmnopqrstuvwxyz
ABCDEFGHIJKLMNOPQRSTUVWXYZ
1234567890 &£$.,:;!?''

abcdefghijklmnopqrstuvwxyz
ABCDEFGHIJKLMNOPQRSTUVWXYZ
1234567890 &£$.,:;!?''

abcdefghijklmnopqrstuvwxyz
ABCDEFGHIJKLMNOPQRSTUVWXYZ
1234567890 &£$.,:;!?''

WTC Favrile

Tom Carnase
World Typeface Center
1985

Autologic, Linotype

Light, light italic, regular, regular italic, medium, medium italic, bold, bold italic

Fourth typeface by the designer for WTC

abcdefghijklmnopqrstuvwxyz
ABCDEFGHIJKLMNOPQRSTUVWXYZ
1234567890 &£.,:;!?''

abcdefghijklmnopqrstuvwxyz
ABCDEFGHIJKLMNOPQRSTUVWXYZ
1234567890 &£.,:;!?''

abcdefghijklmnopqrstuvwxyz
ABCDEFGHIJKLMNOPQRSTUVWXYZ
1234567890 &£.,:;!?''

abcdefghijklmnopqrstuvwxyz
ABCDEFGHIJKLMNOPQRSTUVWXYZ
1234567890 &£.,:;!?''

Fehrle Display

Erich Fehrle
Linotype (Stempel)
1976

One weight only

abcdefghijklmnopqrstuvwxyz
ABCDEFGHIJKLMNOPQRSTUVWXYZ
1234567890 &£$.,:;!?""

Feinan

Henry Mikiewicz
Compugraphic
1983

Light, regular, bold, inline

abcdefghijklmnopqrstuvwxyz
ABCDEFGHIJKLMNOPQRSTUVWXYZ
1234567890 &

abcdefghijklmnopqrstuvwxyz
ABCDEFGHIJKLMNOPQRSTUVWXYZ
1234567890 &

abcdefghijklmnopqrstuvwxyz
ABCDEFGHIJKLMNOPQRSTUVWXYZ
1234567890 &

abcdefghijklmnopqrstuvwxyz
ABCDEFGHIJKLMNOPQRSTUVWXYZ
1234567890 &

ITC Fenice

Aldo Novarese
International Typeface Corporation
1980

Autologic, Berthold, Compugraphic,
Linotype, Monotype, Scangraphic,
Varityper
Industrial 817 (Bitstream)
FE (Itek)

Light, light italic, regular, regular
italic, bold, bold italic, ultra, ultra
italic

Designed originally for H Berthold
AG in 1977

abcdefghijklmnopqrstuvwxyz
ABCDEFGHIJKLMNOPQRSTUVWXYZ
1234567890 1234567890 &£$.,:;!?"

abcdefghijklmnopqrstuvwxyz
ABCDEFGHIJKLMNOPQRSTUVWXYZ
1234567890 &£$.,:;!?"

abcdefghijklmnopqrstuvwxyz
ABCDEFGHIJKLMNOPQRSTUVWXYZ
1234567890 &£$.,:;!?"

abcdefghijklmnopqrstuvwxyz
ABCDEFGHIJKLMNOPQRSTUVWXYZ
1234567890 &£$.,:;!?"

Flange

Leslie Usherwood
Typesettra
1980

Berthold, Scangraphic

Light, light italic, regular, regular
italic, medium, medium italic, bold,
extra bold

abcdefghijklmnopqrstuvwxyz
ABCDEFGHIJKLMNOPQRSTUVWXYZ
1234567890 &£$.,:;!?"

abcdefghijklmnopqrstuvwxyz
ABCDEFGHIJKLMNOPQRSTUVWXYZ
1234567890 &£$.,:;!?"

abcdefghijklmnopqrstuvwxyz
ABCDEFGHIJKLMNOPQRSTUVWXYZ
1234567890 &£$.,:;!?"

abcdefghijklmnopqrstuvwxyz
ABCDEFGHIJKLMNOPQRSTUVWXYZ
1234567890 &£$.,:;!?"

Fleet Titling

John Peters
Monotype
1967

One weight only

ABCDEFGHIJKLMNOPQRSTUVWXYZ&

Flora

Gerard Unger
Hell
1980

Medium, bold

Italic designed to work with Praxis
(q.v.). Idea evolved from Graphik by
F H E Schneidler of 1934 and
experiments by the artist with a
felt-tip pen as a lettering tool.
Released as the first typeface in the
ITC Typographica series in 1989,
along with Isadora (q.v.)

abcdefghijklmnopqrstuvwxyz
ABCDEFGHIJKLMNOPQRSTUVWXYZ
1234567890 1234567890 &£$.,:;!?"

abcdefghijklmnopqrstuvwxyz
ABCDEFGHIJKLMNOPQRSTUVWXYZ
1234567890 1234567890 &£$.,:;!?"

Footlight

Ong Chong Wah
Monotype
1986

Light, light italic, medium, medium
italic, bold, bold italic, extra bold,
extra bold italic

abcdefghijklmnopqrstuvwxyz
ABCDEFGHIJKLMNOPQRSTUVWXYZ
1234567890 .,:;!?"

abcdefghijklmnopqrstuvwxyz
ABCDEFGHIJKLMNOPQRSTUVWXYZ
1234567890 .,:;!?"

abcdefghijklmnopqrstuvwxyz
ABCDEFGHIJKLMNOPQRSTUVWXYZ
1234567890 .,:;!?"

abcdefghijklmnopqrstuvwxyz
ABCDEFGHIJKLMNOPQRSTUVWXYZ
1234567890 .,:;!?"

73

Formata

Bernd Mollenstadt
Berthold
1984

Light, light italic, light condensed, light condensed italic, regular, regular italic, regular condensed, regular condensed italic, medium, medium italic, medium condensed, medium condensed italic, bold, bold italic, bold condensed, bold condensed italic, outline

Condensed versions were added to the family in 1988

abcdefghijklmnopqrstuvwxyz
ABCDEFGHIJKLMNOPQRSTUVWXYZ
1234567890 &£$.,:;!?"

abcdefghijklmnopqrstuvwxyz
ABCDEFGHIJKLMNOPQRSTUVWXYZ
1234567890 &£$.,:;!?"

abcdefghijklmnopqrstuvwxyz
ABCDEFGHIJKLMNOPQRSTUVWXYZ
1234567890 &£$.,:;!?"

abcdefghijklmnopqrstuvwxyz
ABCDEFGHIJKLMNOPQRSTUVWXYZ
1234567890 &£$.,:;!?"

Franco

Linda Hoffman
Varityper
1984

One weight only

Named after Franco Pomi, a principal of the dealership for Varityper in Italy

abcdefghijklmnopqrstuvwxyz
ABCDEFGHIJKLMNOPQRSTUVWXYZ
1234567890 &£$.,:;!?''

abcdefghijklmnopqrstuvwxyz
ABCDEFGHIJKLMNOPQRSTUVWXYZ
1234567890 &£$.,:;!?''

Franklin Antiqua

Günter Gerhard Lange
Berthold
1976

Regular, regular italic, medium,
medium italic, bold

abcdefghijklmnopqrstuvwxyz
ABCDEFGHIJKLMNOPQRSTUVWXYZ
1234567890 &£$.,:;!?"

abcdefghijklmnopqrstuvwxyz
ABCDEFGHIJKLMNOPQRSTUVWXYZ
1234567890 &£$.,:;!?"

abcdefghijklmnopqrstuvwxyz
ABCDEFGHIJKLMNOPQRSTUVWXYZ
1234567890 &£$.,:;!?"

ITC Franklin Gothic

Victor Caruso
International Typeface Corporation
1980

Adobe, Autologic, Berthold,
Compugraphic, Hell, Linotype,
Monotype, Scangraphic, Varityper
Gothic 744 (Bitstream)

Book, book italic, medium, medium
italic, demi, demi italic, heavy,
heavy italic

Based on Franklin Gothic designed
by Morris Fuller Benton for the
American Type Founders Co in 1904

abcdefghijklmnopqrstuvwxyz
ABCDEFGHIJKLMNOPQRSTUVWXYZ
1234567890 &£$.,:;!?"

abcdefghijklmnopqrstuvwxyz
ABCDEFGHIJKLMNOPQRSTUVWXYZ
1234567890 &£$.,:;!?"

abcdefghijklmnopqrstuvwxyz
ABCDEFGHIJKLMNOPQRSTUVWXYZ
1234567890 &£$.,:;!?"

abcdefghijklmnopqrstuvwxyz
ABCDEFGHIJKLMNOPQRSTUVWXYZ
1234567890 &£$.,:;!?"

Friz Quadrata

Ernst Friz
International Typeface Corporation
1978

Adobe, Autologic, Berthold,
Compugraphic, Hell, Linotype,
Monotype, Scangraphic, Varityper
Flareserif 816 (Bitstream)
FZ (Itek)

Regular, bold

Based on Friz Quadrata Regular
designed for the Visual Graphics
Corporation in 1965. Bold styles
drawn by Victor Caruso

abcdefghijklmnopqrstuvwxyz
ABCDEFGHIJKLMNOPQRSTUVWXYZ
1234567890 &£$.,:;!?"

abcdefghijklmnopqrstuvwxyz
ABCDEFGHIJKLMNOPQRSTUVWXYZ
1234567890 &£$.,:;!?"

Frutiger

Adrian Frutiger
Linotype (Stempel)
1976

Adobe, Berthold, Monotype
Provencale (Autologic)
Humanist 777 (Bitstream)
Frontiera (Compugraphic)
Freeborn (Scangraphic)
Siegfried (Varityper)

Light, light italic, medium, medium
italic, bold, bold italic, black, black
italic, ultra black, light condensed,
medium condensed, bold
condensed, black condensed, extra
black condensed

Originally conceived as lettering for
signs at the Charles de Gaulle
Airport in Roissy which opened
during 1975

abcdefghijklmnopqrstuvwxyz
ABCDEFGHIJKLMNOPQRSTUVWXYZ
1234567890 &£$.,:;!?"

abcdefghijklmnopqrstuvwxyz
ABCDEFGHIJKLMNOPQRSTUVWXYZ
1234567890 &£$.,:;!?"

abcdefghijklmnopqrstuvwxyz
ABCDEFGHIJKLMNOPQRSTUVWXYZ
1234567890 &£$.,:;!?"

abcdefghijklmnopqrstuvwxyz
ABCDEFGHIJKLMNOPQRSTUVWXYZ
1234567890 &£$.,:;!?"

For **Galathea** see Supplement

ITC Galliard

Matthew Carter
International Typeface Corporation
1982

Adobe, Autologic, Berthold,
Compugraphic, Hell, Monotype,
Scangraphic, Varityper
Aldine 701 (Bitstream)
GL (Itek)

Roman, italic, bold, bold italic,
black, black italic, ultra, ultra italic

Originally released by Linotype in
1978 and made available under
licence to ITC. Based on a sixteenth-
century design by Robert Granjon

abcdefghijklmnopqrstuvwxyz
ABCDEFGHIJKLMNOPQRSTUVWXYZ
1234567890 1234567890 &£$.,:;!?''

abcdefghijklmnopqrstuvwxyz
ABCDEFGHIJKLMNOPQRSTUVWXYZ
1234567890 &£$.,:;!?''

abcdefghijklmnopqrstuvwxyz
ABCDEFGHIJKLMNOPQRSTUVWXYZ
1234567890 1234567890 &£$.,:;!?''

abcdefghijklmnopqrstuvwxyz
ABCDEFGHIJKLMNOPQRSTUVWXYZ
1234567890 &£$.,:;!?''

ITC Gamma

Jovica Veljovic
International Typeface Corporation
1986

Autologic, Berthold, Compugraphic,
Linotype, Monotype, Scangraphic,
Varityper
GA (Itek)

Book, book italic, medium, medium
italic, bold, bold italic, black, black
italic

Third typeface designed by Jovica
Veljovic for ITC

abcdefghijklmnopqrstuvwxyz
ABCDEFGHIJKLMNOPQRSTUVWXYZ
1234567890 1234567890 &£$.,:;!?''

abcdefghijklmnopqrstuvwxyz
ABCDEFGHIJKLMNOPQRSTUVWXYZ
1234567890 1234567890 &£$.,:;!?''

abcdefghijklmnopqrstuvwxyz
ABCDEFGHIJKLMNOPQRSTUVWXYZ
1234567890 1234567890 &£$.,:;!?''

abcdefghijklmnopqrstuvwxyz
ABCDEFGHIJKLMNOPQRSTUVWXYZ
1234567890 1234567890 &£$.,:;!?''

Gando Ronde

Hans-Jorg Hunziker and Matthew Carter
Linotype (Mergenthaler)
1970

French 111 (Bitstream)

One weight only

Another script designed for phototypesetting in the early days

abcdefghijklmnopqrstuvwxyz
ABCDEFGHIJKLMNOPQRSTUVWXYZ
1234567890 &£$.,:;!?''

Adobe Garamond

Robert Slimbach
Adobe
1989

Regular, regular italic, semi bold, semi bold italic, bold, bold italic, titling capitals

Modelled on original designs researched at the Plantin-Moretus museum in Antwerp

abcdefghijklmnopqrstuvwxyz
ABCDEFGHIJKLMNOPQRSTUVWXYZ
1234567890 1234567890 &£$.,:;!?''

abcdefghijklmnopqrstuvwxyz
ABCDEFGHIJKLMNOPQRSTUVWXYZ
1234567890 1234567890 &£$.,:;!?''

abcdefghijklmnopqrstuvwxyz
ABCDEFGHIJKLMNOPQRSTUVWXYZ
1234567890 1234567890 &£$.,:;!?''

abcdefghijklmnopqrstuvwxyz
ABCDEFGHIJKLMNOPQRSTUVWXYZ
1234567890 1234567890 &£$.,:;!?''

Garamond

Günter Gerhard Lange
Berthold
1972

Regular, regular italic, regular condensed, medium, medium italic, medium condensed, bold

abcdefghijklmnopqrstuvwxyz
ABCDEFGHIJKLMNOPQRSTUVWXYZ
1234567890 1234567890 &£$.,:;!?"

abcdefghijklmnopqrstuvwxyz
ABCDEFGHIJKLMNOPQRSTUVWXYZ
1234567890 1234567890 &£$.,:;!?"

abcdefghijklmnopqrstuvwxyz
ABCDEFGHIJKLMNOPQRSTUVWXYZ
1234567890 1234567890 &£$.,:;!?"

abcdefghijklmnopqrstuvwxyz
ABCDEFGHIJKLMNOPQRSTUVWXYZ
1234567890 &£$.,:;!?"

ITC Garamond

Tony Stan
International Typeface Corporation
1975

Adobe, Autologic, Berthold, Compugraphic, Hell, Linotype, Monotype, Scangraphic, Varityper
Aldine 851 (Bitstream)
GI (Itek)

Light, light italic, book, book italic, bold, bold italic, ultra, ultra italic, light condensed, light condensed italic, book condensed, book condensed italic, bold condensed, bold condensed italic, ultra condensed, ultra condensed italic

Ultra and book weights were released in 1975, followed by the remainder of the family in 1977. In this ITC re-working of a classic sixteenth-century design, Tony Stan took some inspiration from the version issued by Morris Fuller Benton for the American Type Founders Co in 1917

abcdefghijklmnopqrstuvwxyz
ABCDEFGHIJKLMNOPQRSTUVWXYZ
1234567890 &£$.,:;!?"

abcdefghijklmnopqrstuvwxyz
ABCDEFGHIJKLMNOPQRSTUVWXYZ
1234567890 &£$.,:;!?"

abcdefghijklmnopqrstuvwxyz
ABCDEFGHIJKLMNOPQRSTUVWXYZ
1234567890 &£$.,:;!?"

abcdefghijklmnopqrstuvwxyz
ABCDEFGHIJKLMNOPQRSTUVWXYZ
1234567890 &£$.,:;!?"

Garth Graphic

Renee le Winter and Constance
Blanchard
Compugraphic
1979

Regular, regular italic, bold, bold
italic, extra bold, black, regular
condensed, bold condensed

See Matt Antique for the genesis of
this design. Compugraphic acquired
the original artwork around 1976
and the two designers made
revisions and added bold and
condensed versions to the family in
1982. Named after Bill Garth, a co-
founder of the Compugraphic
Corporation

abcdefghijklmnopqrstuvwxyz
ABCDEFGHIJKLMNOPQRSTUVWXYZ
1234567890 &$£—-!?ß,.;:''

abcdefghijklmnopqrstuvwxyz
ABCDEFGHIJKLMNOPQRSTUVWXYZ
1234567890 &$£—-!?ß,.;:''

abcdefghijklmnopqrstuvwxyz
ABCDEFGHIJKLMNOPQRSTUVWXYZ
1234567890 &$£—-!?ß,.;:''

abcdefghijklmnopqrstuvwxyz
ABCDEFGHIJKLMNOPQRSTUVWXYZ
1234567890 &$£—-!?ß,.;:''

Geometrica

Staff designers
Autologic
1985

Titling, initials (outline, cameo, and
normal), constructed initials
(outline, cameo, and normal)

Based on lettering by Fra Luca de
Pacioli, the Italian scribe of the
Renaissance period

ABCDEFGHIJKLMNOP
QRSTUVWXYZ

Gerstner Original

Karl Gerstner
Berthold
1987

Light, light italic, medium, medium italic, demi bold, demi bold italic, bold, bold italic

Typographical engineering of the family was done under the direction of Bernd Mollenstadt at the Munich office of Berthold

abcdefghijklmnopqrstuvwxyz
ABCDEFGHIJKLMNOPQRSTUVWXYZ
1234567890&£$.,!?"

abcdefghijklmnopqrstuvwxyz
ABCDEFGHIJKLMNOPQRSTUVWXYZ
1234567890&£$.,!?"

abcdefghijklmnopqrstuvwxyz
ABCDEFGHIJKLMNOPQRSTUVWXYZ
1234567890&£$.,!?"

abcdefghijklmnopqrstuvwxyz
ABCDEFGHIJKLMNOPQRSTUVWXYZ
1234567890&£$.,!?"

ITC Giovanni

Robert Slimbach
International Typeface Corporation
1989

Berthold, Compugraphic, Linotype, Varityper

Book, book italic, bold, bold italic, black, black italic

Second typeface by the designer for ITC

abcdefghijklmnopqrstuvwxyz
ABCDEFGHIJKLMNOPQRSTUVWXYZ
1234567890 1234567890 &£$.,:;!?"

abcdefghijklmnopqrstuvwxyz
ABCDEFGHIJKLMNOPQRSTUVWXYZ
1234567890 1234567890 &£$.,:;!?"

abcdefghijklmnopqrstuvwxyz
ABCDEFGHIJKLMNOPQRSTUVWXYZ
1234567890 1234567890 &£$.,:;!?"

abcdefghijklmnopqrstuvwxyz
ABCDEFGHIJKLMNOPQRSTUVWXYZ
1234567890 1234567890 &£$.,:;!?"

Glypha

Adrian Frutiger
Linotype (Stempel)
1979

Adobe
Gentleman (Scangraphic)
Pharaoh (Varityper)

Thin, thin italic, light, light italic, regular, regular italic, bold, bold italic, black, black italic

Developed with the aid of the Ikarus digitisation computer program

abcdefghijklmnopqrstuvwxyz
ABCDEFGHIJKLMNOPQRSTUVWXYZ
1234567890 &£$.,:;!?''

abcdefghijklmnopqrstuvwxyz
ABCDEFGHIJKLMNOPQRSTUVWXYZ
1234567890 &£$.,:;!?''

abcdefghijklmnopqrstuvwxyz
ABCDEFGHIJKLMNOPQRSTUVWXYZ
1234567890 &£$.,:;!?''

abcdefghijklmnopqrstuvwxyz
ABCDEFGHIJKLMNOPQRSTUVWXYZ
1234567890 &£$.,:;!?''

ITC Golden Type

Sigrid Engelmann, Helge Jorgensen, Andrew Newton
International Typeface Corporation
1989

Original, bold, black

Based on the Golden Type of William Morris, first used at the Kelmscott Press for the production of *The Golden Legend* in 1892

abcdefghijklmnopqrstuvwxyz
ABCDEFGHIJKLMNOPQRSTUVWXYZ
1234567890 1234567890 &£$.,:;!?''

abcdefghijklmnopqrstuvwxyz
ABCDEFGHIJKLMNOPQRSTUVWXYZ
1234567890 1234567890 &£$.,:;!?''

ITC Gorilla

Tom Carnase and Ronne Bonder
International Typeface Corporation
1970

Berthold, Compugraphic, Linotype, Varityper
Revival 425 (Bitstream)

Roman only

Designed for display composition

aabcdefghhijklmmnnopqrsttuuvwxyz
ABCDEFGHIJKLMMNOPQRRSTUVWXYZ
1234567890 &£$.,:;!?""

WTC Goudy

Tom Carnase
World Typeface Center
1982

Linotype

Light, light italic, regular, regular italic, medium, medium italic, bold, bold italic

Second design issued by the World Typeface Center

abcdefghijklmnopqrstuvwxyz
ABCDEFGHIJKLMNOPQRSTUVWXYZ
1234567890 &£.,:;!?''

abcdefghijklmnopqrstuvwxyz
ABCDEFGHIJKLMNOPQRSTUVWXYZ
1234567890 &£.,:;!?''

abcdefghijklmnopqrstuvwxyz
ABCDEFGHIJKLMNOPQRSTUVWXYZ
1234567890 &£.,:;!?''

abcdefghijklmnopqrstuvwxyz
ABCDEFGHIJKLMNOPQRSTUVWXYZ
1234567890 &£.,:;!?''

ITC Goudy Sans

Frederic W Goudy
International Typeface Corporation
1986

Autologic, Berthold, Compugraphic, Linotype, Scangraphic, Varityper
GN (Itek)

Book, book italic, medium, medium italic, bold, bold italic, black, black italic

Based on a design for the Lanston Monotype Co in 1929. Frederic Goudy ventured into the sanserif genre on only one other occasion with a Lining Gothic of 1921. Compugraphic revived the present typeface and granted a licence to ITC

abcdefghijklmnopqrstuvwxyz
ABCDEFGHIJKLMNOPQRSTUVWXYZ
1234567890 &£$.,:;!?''

abcdefghijklmnopqrstuvwxyz
ABCDEFGHIJKLMNOPQRSTUVWXYZ
1234567890 &£$.,:;!?''

abcdefghijklmnopqrstuvwxyz
ABCDEFGHIJKLMNOPQRSTUVWXYZ
1234567890 &£$.,:;!?''

abcdefghijklmnopqrstuvwxyz
ABCDEFGHIJKLMNOPQRSTUVWXYZ
1234567890 &£$.,:;!?''

ITC Grizzly

Tom Carnase and Ronne Bonder
International Typeface Corporation
1970

Berthold, Compugraphic, Linotype,
Varityper
Geometric 735 (Bitstream)

Roman only

Designed for display composition

aabbcdeefghijjkklmnopqrsstttuvwxyyz
ABCDEFGGHHIJJKKLMNOP
QQRSTUVWWWXYZ
1122345678900 &£$.,:;!?" "

ITC Grouch

Tom Carnase and Ronne Bonder
International Typeface Corporation
1970

Berthold, Compugraphic, Linotype,
Varityper
Dutch 791 (Bitstream)

Roman only

Designed for display composition

abcdefghijjklmnopqrstuvwxyz
ABCDEFGHIJKLMNOPQRSTUVWXYZ
1234567890 &£$.,:;!?""

Guardi

Reinhard Haus
Linotype
1986

Regular, regular italic, bold, bold
italic, black, black italic

abcdefghijklmnopqrstuvwxyz
ABCDEFGHIJKLMNOPQRSTUVWXYZ
1234567890 1234567890 &£$.,:;!?''

abcdefghijklmnopqrstuvwxyz
ABCDEFGHIJKLMNOPQRSTUVWXYZ
1234567890 1234567890 &£$.,:;!?''

abcdefghijklmnopqrstuvwxyz
ABCDEFGHIJKLMNOPQRSTUVWXYZ
1234567890 1234567890 &£$.,:;!?''

abcdefghijklmnopqrstuvwxyz
ABCDEFGHIJKLMNOPQRSTUVWXYZ
1234567890 1234567890 &£$.,:;!?''

Hanseatic

Staff designers
Linotype (Stempel)
1965

One weight only

abcdefghijklmnopqrstuvwxyz
ABCDEFGHIJKLMNOPQRSTUVWXYZ
1234567890 &£$.,:;!?"

Heldustry

Phil Martin
TypeSpectra
1978

Compugraphic, Linotype

Regular, regular italic, medium,
medium italic, demi bold, demi bold
italic

abcdefghijklmnopqrstuvwxyz
ABCDEFGHIJKLMNOPQRSTUVWXYZ
1234567890 &£.,:;!?"

abcdefghijklmnopqrstuvwxyz
ABCDEFGHIJKLMNOPQRSTUVWXYZ
1234567890 &£.,:;!?"

abcdefghijklmnopqrstuvwxyz
ABCDEFGHIJKLMNOPQRSTUVWXYZ
1234567890 &£.,:;!?"

abcdefghijklmnopqrstuvwxyz
ABCDEFGHIJKLMNOPQRSTUVWXYZ
1234567890 &£.,:;!?"

For **Helicon** see Supplement

Helserif

Ed Kelton
Alphabet Innovations
1976

Linotype

Light, light italic, regular, medium,
bold, open, shaded, contour

abcdefghijklmnopqrstuvwxyz
ABCDEFGHIJKLMNOPQRSTUVWXYZ
1234567890 &£$.,:;!?"

abcdefghijklmnopqrstuvwxyz
ABCDEFGHIJKLMNOPQRSTUVWXYZ
1234567890 &£$.,:;!?"

abcdefghijklmnopqrstuvwxyz
ABCDEFGHIJKLMNOPQRSTUVWXYZ
1234567890 &£$.,:;!?"

abcdefghijklmnopqrstuvwxyz
ABCDEFGHIJKLMNOPQRSTUVWXYZ
1234567890 &£$.,:;!?"

Helvetica Rounded

Staff designers
Linotype (Stempel)
1978

Monotype
Geneva Roundhand (Autologic)
AG Buch Rounded (Berthold)
Helios Rounded (Compugraphic)

Bold, bold italic, bold condensed,
bold outline, black, black italic

abcdefghijklmnopqrstuvwxyz
ABCDEFGHIJKLMNOPQRSTUVWXYZ
1234567890 &£$.,:;!?"'

abcdefghijklmnopqrstuvwxyz
ABCDEFGHIJKLMNOPQRSTUVWXYZ
1234567890 &£$.,:;!?"'

Henche

Robert Stefanic
Varityper
1984

One weight only

Named after the dealer for Varityper
in Spain

abcdefghijklmnopqrstuvwxyz
ABCDEFGHIJKLMNOPQRSTUVWXYZ
1234567890 &£$.,:;!?"'

abcdefghijklmnopqrstuvwxyz
ABCDEFGHIJKLMNOPQRSTUVWXYZ
1234567890 &£$.,:;!?"'

Hiroshige

Cynthia Hollandsworth
AlphaOmega Typography
1986

Adobe, Compugraphic, Linotype

Book, book italic, medium, medium italic, bold, bold italic, black, black italic

Specially commissioned by George Braziller, the New York publisher, for the book *One Hundred Famous Views of Edo.* Subject of the volume was a collection of nineteenth-century woodblocks, discovered in the library of the Brooklyn Museum, by the Japanese artist Hiroshige

abcdefghijklmnopqrstuvwxyz
ABCDEFGHIJKLMNOPQRSTUVWXYZ
1234567890 &£$.,:;!?''

abcdefghijklmnopqrstuvwxyz
ABCDEFGHIJKLMNOPQRSTUVWXYZ
1234567890 &£$.,:;!?''

abcdefghijklmnopqrstuvwxyz
ABCDEFGHIJKLMNOPQRSTUVWXYZ
1234567890 &£$.,:;!?''

abcdefghijklmnopqrstuvwxyz
ABCDEFGHIJKLMNOPQRSTUVWXYZ
1234567890 &£$.,:;!?''

Hollander

Gerard Unger
Hell
1983

Scangraphic

Regular, regular italic, bold

abcdefghijklmnopqrstuvwxyz
ABCDEFGHIJKLMNOPQRSTUVWXYZ
1234567890 1234567890 &£$.,:;!?''

abcdefghijklmnopqrstuvwxyz
ABCDEFGHIJKLMNOPQRSTUVWXYZ
1234567890 1234567890 &£$.,:;!?''

abcdefghijklmnopqrstuvwxyz
ABCDEFGHIJKLMNOPQRSTUVWXYZ
1234567890 1234567890 &£$.,:;!?''

Holland Seminar

Hollis Holland
Compugraphic
1974

Dutch Roman (Varityper)

Roman and italic

Another design from the same
source is Holland Title shown here
as the third example

abcdefghijklmnopqrstuvwxyz
ABCDEFGHIJKLMNOPQRSTUVWXYZ
1234567890 & $£—-!?ß,.;:''

abcdefghijklmnopqrstuvwxyz
ABCDEFGHIJKLMNOPQRSTUVWXYZ
1234567890 & $£—-!?ß,.;:''

abcdefghijklmnopqrstuvwxyz
ABCDEFGHIJKLMNOPQRSTUVWXYZ
1234567890 & $£—-!?ß,.;:''

ITC Honda

Tom Carnase and Ronne Bonner
International Typeface Corporation
1970

Autologic, Berthold, Compugraphic,
Varityper

Roman only

Designed for display composition

aabcdeffgghijkklmnopqrrssttuvwxyyz
ABCDEFGHIJKLMNOPQRSTUVWXYZ
1234567890 &$.,:;!?""

Icone

Adrian Frutiger
Linotype
1980

Monotype

Light, light italic, medium, medium italic, bold, bold italic, extra black, extra black italic, bold outline

abcdefghijklmnopqrstuvwxyz
ABCDEFGHIJKLMNOPQRSTUVWXYZ
1234567890 1234567890 &£$.,:;!?''

abcdefghijklmnopqrstuvwxyz
ABCDEFGHIJKLMNOPQRSTUVWXYZ
1234567890 1234567890 &£$.,:;!?''

abcdefghijklmnopqrstuvwxyz
ABCDEFGHIJKLMNOPQRSTUVWXYZ
1234567890 1234567890 &£$.,:;!?''

abcdefghijklmnopqrstuvwxyz
ABCDEFGHIJKLMNOPQRSTUVWXYZ
1234567890 &£$.,:;!?''

Imago

Günter Gerhard Lange
Berthold
1982

Light, light italic, book, book italic, medium, medium italic, extra bold, extra bold italic

abcdefghijklmnopqrstuvwxyz
ABCDEFGHIJKLMNOPQRSTUVWXYZ
1234567890 &£$.,:;!?''

abcdefghijklmnopqrstuvwxyz
ABCDEFGHIJKLMNOPQRSTUVWXYZ
1234567890 &£$.,:;!?''

abcdefghijklmnopqrstuvwxyz
ABCDEFGHIJKLMNOPQRSTUVWXYZ
1234567890 &£$.,:;!?''

abcdefghijklmnopqrstuvwxyz
ABCDEFGHIJKLMNOPQRSTUVWXYZ
1234567890 &£$.,:;!?''

Impressum

Konrad Bauer and Walter Baum
Bauer (Neufville)
1963

Adobe, Berthold, Compugraphic,
Hell, Linotype

Light, light italic, medium, medium
italic, semi bold, semi bold italic,
bold, bold italic

abcdefghijklmnopqrstuvwxyz
ABCDEFGHIJKLMNOPQRSTUVWXYZ
1234567890 &£$.,:;!?''

abcdefghijklmnopqrstuvwxyz
ABCDEFGHIJKLMNOPQRSTUVWXYZ
1234567890 &£$.,:;!?''

abcdefghijklmnopqrstuvwxyz
ABCDEFGHIJKLMNOPQRSTUVWXYZ
1234567890 &£$.,:;!?''

Industria

Neville Brody
Linotype
1989

Solid, inline

Suitable for display composition
only

abcdefghijklmnopqrstuvwxyz
ABCDEFGHIJKLMNOPQRSTUVWXYZ
1234567890 &£$.,:;!?''

abcdefghijklmnopqrstuvwxyz
ABCDEFGHIJKLMNOPQRSTUVWXYZ
1234567890 &£$.,:;!?''

Iridium

Adrian Frutiger
Linotype (Stempel)
1972

Iron (Scangraphic)

Medium, medium italic, bold

abcdefghijklmnopqrstuvwxyz
ABCDEFGHIJKLMNOPQRSTUVWXYZ
1234567890 &£$.,:;!?"

abcdefghijklmnopqrstuvwxyz
ABCDEFGHIJKLMNOPQRSTUVWXYZ
1234567890 &£$.,:;!?"

abcdefghijklmnopqrstuvwxyz
ABCDEFGHIJKLMNOPQRSTUVWXYZ
1234567890 &£$.,:;!?"

Adobe Ironwood

Anonymous
Adobe
1990

One weight only

Based on an early American design
for wood letter

ABCDEFGHIJKLMNOPQRSTUVWXYZ
1234567890 &£$.,:;!?"

Isadora

Kris Holmes
Hell
1985

Regular, bold

Adopted by ITC and released in
1989 as first in the Typographica
series along with Flora (q.v.).
Named after Isadora Duncan, the
dancer

abcdefghijklmnopqrstuvwxyz
ABCDEFGHIJKLMNOPQRSTUVWXYZ
1234567890 1234567890 &£$.,:;!?"

abcdefghijklmnopqrstuvwxyz
ABCDEFGHIJKLMNOPQRSTUVWXYZ
1234567890 1234567890 &£$.,:;!?"

ITC Isbell

Dick Isbell and Jerry Campbell
International Typeface Corporation
1981

Autologic, Berthold, Compugraphic,
Linotype, Monotype, Scangraphic,
Varityper
Revival 821 (Bitstream)
IS (Itek)

Book, book italic, medium, medium
italic, bold, bold italic, heavy, heavy
italic

Campbell-Isbell Alphabets was
established by the two designers
during 1975 to service advertising
agencies and studios

abcdefghijklmnopqrstuvwxyz
ABCDEFGHIJKLMNOPQRSTUVWXYZ
1234567890 &£$.,:;!?"

*abcdefghijklmnopqrstuvwxyz
ABCDEFGHIJKLMNOPQRSTUVWXYZ
1234567890 &£$.,:;!?"*

**abcdefghijklmnopqrstuvwxyz
ABCDEFGHIJKLMNOPQRSTUVWXYZ
1234567890 &£$.,:;!?"**

***abcdefghijklmnopqrstuvwxyz
ABCDEFGHIJKLMNOPQRSTUVWXYZ
1234567890 &£$.,:;!?"***

Italia

Colin Brignall
International Typeface Corporation
1977

Adobe, Autologic, Berthold,
Compugraphic, Linotype,
Monotype, Scangraphic, Varityper
Revival 791 (Bitstream)
IT (Itek)

Book, medium, bold

Designed originally for Letraset in
1975 and licensed two years later to
ITC. In 1979 a Medium Condensed
style was added by Letraset for
transfer lettering

abcdefghijklmnopqrstuvwxyz
ABCDEFGHIJKLMNOPQRSTUVWXYZ
1234567890 &£$.,:;!?"

**abcdefghijklmnopqrstuvwxyz
ABCDEFGHIJKLMNOPQRSTUVWXYZ
1234567890 &£$.,:;!?"**

Jaeger-Antiqua

Gustav Jaeger
Berthold
1984

Light, light italic, regular, regular italic, medium, medium italic, bold, bold italic

abcdefghijklmnopqrstuvwxyz
ABCDEFGHIJKLMNOPQRSTUVWXYZ
1234567890 &£$.,:;!?"

abcdefghijklmnopqrstuvwxyz
ABCDEFGHIJKLMNOPQRSTUVWXYZ
1234567890 &£$.,:;!?"

abcdefghijklmnopqrstuvwxyz
ABCDEFGHIJKLMNOPQRSTUVWXYZ
1234567890 &£$.,:;!?"

abcdefghijklmnopqrstuvwxyz
ABCDEFGHIJKLMNOPQRSTUVWXYZ
1234567890 &£$.,:;!?"

ITC Jamille

Mark Jamra
International Typeface Corporation
1988

Berthold, Compugraphic, Linotype, Monotype, Varityper

Book, book italic, bold, bold italic, black, black italic

Released originally for use in 1987 on equipment manufactured by Dr-Ing Rudolph Hell GmbH and made available under licence to ITC

abcdefghijklmnopqrstuvwxyz
ABCDEFGHIJKLMNOPQRSTUVWXYZ
1234567890 1234567890 &£$.,:;!?''

abcdefghijklmnopqrstuvwxyz
ABCDEFGHIJKLMNOPQRSTUVWXYZ
1234567890 &£$.,:;!?''

abcdefghijklmnopqrstuvwxyz
ABCDEFGHIJKLMNOPQRSTUVWXYZ
1234567890 1234567890 &£$.,:;!?''

abcdefghijklmnopqrstuvwxyz
ABCDEFGHIJKLMNOPQRSTUVWXYZ
1234567890 &£$.,:;!?''

93

Janson Text

Staff designers
Linotype
1985

Adobe

Regular, regular italic, bold, bold italic, black, black italic

Based on the original Stempel 14-point hand-cast types of 1919 after the design of Nicholas Kis in 1690. Present version was supervised by Professor Horst Heiderhoff in consultation with Adrian Frutiger

abcdefghijklmnopqrstuvwxyz
ABCDEFGHIJKLMNOPQRSTUVWXYZ
1234567890 1234567890 &£$.,:;!?"

abcdefghijklmnopqrstuvwxyz
ABCDEFGHIJKLMNOPQRSTUVWXYZ
1234567890 1234567890 &£$.,:;!?"

abcdefghijklmnopqrstuvwxyz
ABCDEFGHIJKLMNOPQRSTUVWXYZ
1234567890 1234567890 &£$.,:;!?"

abcdefghijklmnopqrstuvwxyz
ABCDEFGHIJKLMNOPQRSTUVWXYZ
1234567890 1234567890 &£$.,:;!?"

Jersey

Gustav Jaeger
Berthold
1985

Regular, regular italic, medium, medium italic, bold, bold italic, extra bold, extra bold italic

abcdefghijklmnopqrstuvwxyz
ABCDEFGHIJKLMNOPQRSTUVWXYZ
1234567890 &£$.,:;!?"

abcdefghijklmnopqrstuvwxyz
ABCDEFGHIJKLMNOPQRSTUVWXYZ
1234567890 &£$.,:;!?"

abcdefghijklmnopqrstuvwxyz
ABCDEFGHIJKLMNOPQRSTUVWXYZ
1234567890 &£$.,:;!?"

abcdefghijklmnopqrstuvwxyz
ABCDEFGHIJKLMNOPQRSTUVWXYZ
1234567890 &£$.,:;!?"

Jumbo

Gustav Jaeger
Berthold
1973

Regular, regular italic

JUMBO

JUMBO

Adobe Juniper

Anonymous
Adobe
1990

One weight only

Based on an early American design
for wood letter

ABCDEFGHIJKLMNOPQRSTUVWXYZ
1234567890 &£$.,:;!?"

ITC Kabel

Staff designers
International Typeface Corporation
1976

Adobe, Autologic, Berthold,
Compugraphic, Linotype,
Monotype, Scangraphic, Varityper
Geometric 731 (Bitstream)
KL (Itek)

Book, medium, demi, bold, ultra,
outline

Based on a design of 1927 by Rudolf
Koch for the Klingspor typefoundry,
an organisation that ceased trading
in 1956. Rights to the Kabel design
subsequently passed to D Stempel
AG which licensed the present
version by ITC

abcdefghijklmnopqrstuvwxyz
ABCDEFGHIJKLMNOPQRSTUVWXYZ
1234567890 &£$.,:;!?"

abcdefghijklmnopqrstuvwxyz
ABCDEFGHIJKLMNOPQRSTUVWXYZ
1234567890 &£$.,:;!?"

Kapitellia

Wulf Jarosch
Hell
1974

Bold weight only

abcdefghijklmnopqrstuvwxyz
ABCDEFGHIJKLMNOPQRSTUVWXYZ
1234567890 ß£$.,:;!?"

95

Kis-Janson

Staff designers
Autologic
1985

Regular, regular italic, medium,
medium italic, bold, bold italic

abcdefghijklmnopqrstuvwxyz
ABCDEFGHIJKLMNOPQRSTUVWXYZ
1234567890 &£$.,:;!?"

abcdefghijklmnopqrstuvwxyz
ABCDEFGHIJKLMNOPQRSTUVWXYZ
1234567890 &£$.,:;!?"

abcdefghijklmnopqrstuvwxyz
ABCDEFGHIJKLMNOPQRSTUVWXYZ
1234567890 &£$.,:;!?"

abcdefghijklmnopqrstuvwxyz
ABCDEFGHIJKLMNOPQRSTUVWXYZ
1234567890 &£$.,:;!?"

ITC Korinna

Edward Benguiat and Victor Caruso
International Typeface Corporation
1974

Adobe, Autologic, Berthold,
Compugraphic, Hell, Linotype,
Monotype, Scangraphic, Varityper
Stubserif 711 (Bitstream)
KN (Itek)

Regular, regular kursiv, bold, bold
kursiv, extra bold, extra bold kursiv,
heavy, heavy kursiv, bold outline

Based on Korinna Regular and Bold
cut originally by the typefoundry of
H Berthold AG in 1904. Cursive
versions were added to the family in
1988 as drawn by Ed Benguiat

abcdefghijklmnopqrstuvwxyz
ABCDEFGHIJKLMNOPQRSTUVWXYZ
1234567890 &£$.,:;!?"

abcdefghijklmnopqrstuvwxyz
ABCDEFGHIJKLMNOPQRSTUVWXYZ
1234567890 &£$.,:;!?"

abcdefghijklmnopqrstuvwxyz
ABCDEFGHIJKLMNOPQRSTUVWXYZ
1234567890 &£$.,:;!?"

abcdefghijklmnopqrstuvwxyz
ABCDEFGHIJKLMNOPQRSTUVWXYZ
1234567890 &£$.,:;!?"

Kursivschrift

Staff designers
Berthold
1988

Light, light italic, regular, regular
italic, reclining

abcdefghijklmnopqrstuvwxyz
ABCDEFGHIJKLMNOPQRSTUVWXYZ
1234567890 &£$.,!?''

abcdefghijklmnopqrstuvwxyz
ABCDEFGHIJKLMNOPQRSTUVWXYZ
1234567890 &£$.,!?''

abcdefghijklmnopqrstuvwxyz
ABCDEFGHIJKLMNOPQRSTUVWXYZ
1234567890 &£$.,!?''

abcdefghijklmnopqrstuvwxyz
ABCDEFGHIJKLMNOPQRSTUVWXYZ
1234567890 &£$.,!?''

Lapidar

Aldo Novarese
Berthold
1977

One weight only

abcdefghijklmnopqrstuvwxyz
ABCDEFGHIJKLMNOPQRSTUVWXYZ
1234567890 &£$.,:;!?"

Las Vegas

Georg Kuhn
Linotype (Stempel)
1981

One weight only

abcdefghijklmnopqrstuvwxyz
ABCDEFGHIJKLMNOPQRSTUVWXYZ
1234567890 &£$.,:;!?"

LCD

Staff designers
Berthold
1984

Varityper

One weight only

One of several alphabets imitating
liquid crystal displays. Another is by
Alan Birch for Letraset

ABCDEFGHIJKLMNOPQRSTUVWXYZ
1234567890 &£$.,!?"

Leamington

Adrian Williams
Fonts/Ingrama SA
1978

Autologic, Linotype, Scangraphic

Regular, regular italic, medium,
bold, black

Conceived as a companion text face
for Worcester Round (q.v.)

abcdefghijklmnopqrstuvwxyz
ABCDEFGHIJKLMNOPQRSTUVWXYZ
1234567890 &£$.,:;!?"

abcdefghijklmnopqrstuvwxyz
ABCDEFGHIJKLMNOPQRSTUVWXYZ
1234567890 &£$.,:;!?"

abcdefghijklmnopqrstuvwxyz
ABCDEFGHIJKLMNOPQRSTUVWXYZ
1234567890 &£$.,:;!?"

ITC Leawood

Leslie Usherwood
International Typeface Corporation
1985

Autologic, Berthold, Compugraphic,
Linotype, Scangraphic, Varityper

Book, book italic, medium, medium
italic, bold, bold italic, black, black
italic

Second typeface by this designer for
ITC, the first was ITC Usherwood in
1984. Two intermediate weights in
the family were extrapolated with a
computer-aided design system

abcdefghijklmnopqrstuvwxyz
ABCDEFGHIJKLMNOPQRSTUVWXYZ
1234567890 &£$.,:;!?''

abcdefghijklmnopqrstuvwxyz
ABCDEFGHIJKLMNOPQRSTUVWXYZ
1234567890 &£$.,:;!?''

abcdefghijklmnopqrstuvwxyz
ABCDEFGHIJKLMNOPQRSTUVWXYZ
1234567890 &£$.,:;!?''

abcdefghijklmnopqrstuvwxyz
ABCDEFGHIJKLMNOPQRSTUVWXYZ
1234567890 &£$.,:;!?''

Lectura

Dick Dooijes
Lettergietterij Amsterdam
1969

Berthold, Linotype, Scangraphic,
Varityper
LE (Itek)

Regular, regular italic, medium, bold
condensed

abcdefghijklmnopqrstuvwxyz
ABCDEFGHIJKLMNOPQRSTUVWXYZ
1234567890 &£.,:;!?''

abcdefghijklmnopqrstuvwxyz
ABCDEFGHIJKLMNOPQRSTUVWXYZ
1234567890 &£.,:;!?''

abcdefghijklmnopqrstuvwxyz
ABCDEFGHIJKLMNOPQRSTUVWXYZ
1234567890 &£.,:;!?''

abcdefghijklmnopqrstuvwxyz
ABCDEFGHIJKLMNOPQRSTUVWXYZ
1234567890 &£.,:;!?''

Life

W Bilz and F Simoncini
Simoncini
1965

Adobe, Autologic, Berthold,
Linotype, Scangraphic
Fredonia (Varityper)

Regular, regular italic, bold

abcdefghijklmnopqrstuvwxyz
ABCDEFGHJKLMNOPQRSTUVWXYZ
1234567890 &£$.,:;!?"

abcdefghijklmnopqrstuvwxyz
ABCDEFGHJKLMNOPQRSTUVWXYZ
1234567890 &£$.,:;!?"

abcdefghijklmnopqrstuvwxyz
ABCDEFGHJKLMNOPQRSTUVWXYZ
1234567890 &£$.,:;!?"

Adobe Lithos

Carol Twombly
Adobe
1989

Extra light, light, regular, bold,
black

ABCDEFGHIJKLMNOPQRSTUVWXYZ
1234567890 &£$.,:;!?˘

ABCDEFGHIJKLMNOPQRSTUVWXYZ
1234567890 &£$.,:;!?˘

Lo-Type

Erik Spiekermann
Berthold
1980

Light, regular, medium, medium
italic, bold, bold condensed

Based on an original design by Louis
Oppenheim of 1913

abcdefghijklmnopqrstuvwxyz
ABCDEFGHIJKLMNOPQRSTUVWXYZ
1234567890 &£$.,:;!?"

abcdefghijklmnopqrstuvwxyz
ABCDEFGHIJKLMNOPQRSTUVWXYZ
1234567890 &£$.,:;!?"

ITC Lubalin Graph

Herb Lubalin
International Typeface Corporation
1974

Adobe, Autologic, Berthold,
Compugraphic, Hell, Linotype,
Monotype, Scangraphic, Varityper
Geometric Slabserif 761 (Bitstream)
LG (Itek)

Extra light, extra light oblique,
book, book oblique, medium,
medium oblique, demi, demi
oblique, bold, bold oblique

Lubalin Graph is essentially a
serifed version of Avant Garde
(q.v.). Herb Lubalin designed the
roman styles which were drawn by
Antonio DiSpigna and Joe Sundwall.
Oblique version, drawn by Edward
Benguiat, became available in 1981

abcdefghijklmnopqrstuvwxyz
ABCDEFGHIJKLMNOPQRSTUVWXYZ
1234567890 &£$.,:;!?''

abcdefghijklmnopqrstuvwxyz
ABCDEFGHIJKLMNOPQRSTUVWXYZ
1234567890 &£$.,:;!?''

abcdefghijklmnopqrstuvwxyz
ABCDEFGHIJKLMNOPQRSTUVWXYZ
1234567890 &£$.,:;!?''

abcdefghijklmnopqrstuvwxyz
ABCDEFGHIJKLMNOPQRSTUVWXYZ
1234567890 &£$.,:;!?''

Lucida

Charles Bigelow and Kris Holmes
Bigelow & Holmes
1985

Adobe

Regular, regular italic, bold, sans
regular, sans regular italic, sans
bold

First original typeface designed for
use on low-resolution laser printers.
Pellucida, a series of bitmap display
screen founts, was conceived as a
companion to Lucida. Other
variations of Lucida have been
produced, such as Lucida
Typewriter (1986) and Lucida Bright
(q.v.) for the *Scientific American*
magazine (1987/88)

abcdefghijklmnopqrstuvwxyz
ABCDEFGHIJKLMNOPQRSTUVWXYZ
1234567890 &£$%*.,:;!?"()[]{}

abcdefghijklmnopqrstuvwxyz
ABCDEFGHIJKLMNOPQRSTUVWXYZ
1234567890 &£$%*.,:;!?"()[]{}

abcdefghijklmnopqrstuvwxyz
ABCDEFGHIJKLMNOPQRSTUVWXYZ
1234567890 &£$%*.,:;!?"()[]{}

abcdefghijklmnopqrstuvwxyz
ABCDEFGHIJKLMNOPQRSTUVWXYZ
1234567890 &$%*.,:;!?"()[]

Lucida Bright

Charles Bigelow and Kris Holmes
Bigelow & Holmes
1987

Roman, italic, demi bold, demi bold italic

Designed for setting the *Scientific American* magazine

abcdefghijklmnopqrstuvwxyz
ABCDEFGHIJKLMNOPQRSTUVWXYZ
1234567890 &£$.,:;!?"

abcdefghijklmnopqrstuvwxyz
ABCDEFGHIJKLMNOPQRSTUVWXYZ
1234567890 &£$.,:;!?"

abcdefghijklmnopqrstuvwxyz
ABCDEFGHIJKLMNOPQRSTUVWXYZ
1234567890 &£$.,:;!?"

abcdefghijklmnopqrstuvwxyz
ABCDEFGHIJKLMNOPQRSTUVWXYZ
1234567890 &£$.,:;!?"

Lynton

Leslie Usherwood
Typesettra
1980

Berthold

Light, light italic, light condensed, light condensed italic, regular, regular condensed, bold, bold condensed

abcdefghijklmnopqrstuvwxyz
ABCDEFGHIJKLMNOPQRSTUVWXYZ
1234567890 &£$.,:;!?"

abcdefghijklmnopqrstuvwxyz
ABCDEFGHIJKLMNOPQRSTUVWXYZ
1234567890 &£$.,:;!?"

ITC Machine

Tom Carnase and Ronne Bonder
International Typeface Corporation
1970

Adobe, Autologic, Berthold, Compugraphic, Hell, Linotype, Scangraphic, Varityper
Square 880 (Bitstream)

Regular, bold

ABCDEFGHIJJKLMNOPQRSTUVWXYZ
1234567890 &£$.,:;!?""

Magna Carta

Vladimir Andrich
Alphatype
1974

Regular, regular italic, demi bold,
bold

abcdefghijklmnopqrstuvwxyz
ABCDEFGHIJKLMNOPQRSTUVWXYZ
1234567890 1234567890 &£$.,:;!?''

abcdefghijklmnopqrstuvwxyz
ABCDEFGHIJKLMNOPQRSTUVWXYZ
1234567890 &£$.,:;!?''

abcdefghijklmnopqrstuvwxyz
ABCDEFGHIJKLMNOPQRSTUVWXYZ
1234567890 &£$.,:;!?''

abcdefghijklmnopqrstuvwxyz
ABCDEFGHIJKLMNOPQRSTUVWXYZ
1234567890 &£$.,:;!?''

Mainorm

Karlheinz Maireder
Berthold
1986

Light, bold

abcdefghijklmnopqrstuvwxyz
ABCDEFGHIJKLMNOPQRSTUVWXYZ
1234567890 &£$.,:;!?''

abcdefghijklmnopqrstuvwxyz
ABCDEFGHIJKLMNOPQRSTUVWXYZ
1234567890 &£$.,:;!?''

103

Majora

Ferdinay Duman
Hell
1989

Regular, regular italic, semi bold, semi bold italic, bold, bold italic

abcdefghijklmnopqrstuvwxyz
ABCDEFGHIJKLMNOPQRSTUVWXYZ
1234567890 &£$.,:;!?"'

abcdefghijklmnopqrstuvwxyz
ABCDEFGHIJKLMNOPQRSTUVWXYZ
1234567890 &£$.,:;!?"'

abcdefghijklmnopqrstuvwxyz
ABCDEFGHIJKLMNOPQRSTUVWXYZ
1234567890 &£$.,:;!?"'

abcdefghijklmnopqrstuvwxyz
ABCDEFGHIJKLMNOPQRSTUVWXYZ
1234567890 &£$.,:;!?"'

Marbrook

Leslie Usherwood
Berthold
1983

Light, light italic, book, book italic, regular, regular italic, demi bold, demi bold italic, extra bold, extra bold italic

abcdefghijklmnopqrstuvwxyz
ABCDEFGHIJKLMNOPQRSTUVWXYZ
1234567890 &£$.,:;!?"

abcdefghijklmnopqrstuvwxyz
ABCDEFGHIJKLMNOPQRSTUVWXYZ
1234567890 &£$.,:;!?"

abcdefghijklmnopqrstuvwxyz
ABCDEFGHIJKLMNOPQRSTUVWXYZ
1234567890 &£$.,:;!?"

abcdefghijklmnopqrstuvwxyz
ABCDEFGHIJKLMNOPQRSTUVWXYZ
1234567890 &£$.,:;!?"

Marconi

Hermann Zapf
Hell
1975

Book, book italic, semi bold, semi bold italic

First typeface produced with the aid of the Ikarus computer-aided design and digitising system. Some argue the first typeface ever conceived for digital typesetting

abcdefghijklmnopqrstuvwxyz
ABCDEFGHIJKLMNOPQRSTUVWXYZ
1234567890 1234567890 &£$.,:;!?"

abcdefghijklmnopqrstuvwxyz
ABCDEFGHIJKLMNOPQRSTUVWXYZ
1234567890 &£$.,:;!?"

abcdefghijklmnopqrstuvwxyz
ABCDEFGHIJKLMNOPQRSTUVWXYZ
1234567890 &£$.,:;!?"

abcdefghijklmnopqrstuvwxyz
ABCDEFGHIJKLMNOPQRSTUVWXYZ
1234567890 &£$.,:;!?"

Martin Gothic

Phil Martin
Alphabet Innovations
1981

Linotype

Light, light italic, medium, medium italic, bold, bold italic

abcdefghijklmnopqrstuvwxyz
ABCDEFGHIJKLMNOPQRSTUVWXYZ
1234567890 &£$.,:;!?"

abcdefghijklmnopqrstuvwxyz
ABCDEFGHIJKLMNOPQRSTUVWXYZ
1234567890 &£$.,:;!?"

abcdefghijklmnopqrstuvwxyz
ABCDEFGHIJKLMNOPQRSTUVWXYZ
1234567890 &£$.,:;!?"

abcdefghijklmnopqrstuvwxyz
ABCDEFGHIJKLMNOPQRSTUVWXYZ
1234567890 &£$.,:;!?"

For **Marigold** see Supplement

Matt Antique

John Matt
Itek
1980

Medium, medium italic, bold

Originally designed in the 1960s for the ill-fated ATF Typesetter, a photocomposition system that was bedevilled by technical problems. John Matt worked for a time as a staff designer with Itek which accounts for the release of the typeface by that company. See Garth Graphic

abcdefghijklmnopqrstuvwxyz
ABCDEFGHIJKLMNOPQRSTUVWXYZ
1234567890 &£$.,:;!?"

abcdefghijklmnopqrstuvwxyz
ABCDEFGHIJKLMNOPQRSTUVWXYZ
1234567890 &£$.,:;!?"

abcdefghijklmnopqrstuvwxyz
ABCDEFGHIJKLMNOPQRSTUVWXYZ
1234567890 &£$.,:;!?"

Maximus

Walter Tracy
Linotype
1967

Monotype

Roman, bold

First installed for classified advertising at *The Daily Telegraph* newspaper in London during December 1967. It was designed to work optimally at 4¾ point

abcdefghijklmnopqrstuvwxyz
ABCDEFGHIJKLMNOPQRSTUVWXYZ
1234567890 &£$.,:;!?''

Media

André Gürtler, Christian Mengelt,
and Erich Gschwind
Autologic
1976

Regular, regular italic, regular
condensed, medium, medium italic,
medium condensed, bold, bold
condensed

Initially released by BobstGraphic,
the first original typeface to be
developed by that company.
Autologic subsequently acquired
the business in 1981

abcdefghijklmnopqrstuvwxyz
ABCDEFGHIJKLMNOPQRSTUVWXYZ
1234567890 &£$.,:;!?''

abcdefghijklmnopqrstuvwxyz
ABCDEFGHIJKLMNOPQRSTUVWXYZ
1234567890 &£$.,:;!?''

abcdefghijklmnopqrstuvwxyz
ABCDEFGHIJKLMNOPQRSTUVWXYZ
1234567890 &£$.,:;!?''

abcdefghijklmnopqrstuvwxyz
ABCDEFGHIJKLMNOPQRSTUVWXYZ
1234567890 &£$.,:;!?''

Medici Script

Hermann Zapf
Linotype (Stempel)
1971

Cosimo Script (Autologic)

One weight only

abcdefghijklmnopqrstuvwxyz
ABCDEFGHIJKLMNOPQRSTUVWXYZ
1234567890 &£$.,:;!?''

Melencolia

Staff designers
Autologic
1985

Titling, initials (outline, cameo, and
normal), constructed initials
(outline, cameo, and normal)

Based on lettering by Albrecht
Dürer, the German woodcut artist of
the fifteenth and sixteenth centuries

ABCDEFGHIJKLMNOP
QRSTUVWXYZ

ABCDEFGHIJKLMNOP
QRSTUVWXYZ

ABCDEF GHI JKL MNOP
QR S TUVWXYZ

ABCDEFGHIJKLMNOP
QRSTUVWXYZ

ABCDEF GHI JKL MNOP
QR S TUVWXYZ

Adobe Mesquite

Anonymous
Adobe
1990

One weight only

Based on an early American design
for wood letter

ABCDEFGHIJKLMNOPQRSTUVWXYZ
1234567890 &£$.,.:;!?"

ITC Milano Roman

Tom Carnase and Ronne Bonder
International Typeface Corporation
1970

Berthold, Compugraphic

One weight only

abcdefghiijkkllmnopqrstuvvwwxyyz
ABCDEFGHIJKKLMNNOPQRRSTUVWXYZ
1234567890   &ß$.,:;!?""

For **Mikaway** see Supplement

Adobe Minion

Robert Slimbach
Adobe
1990

Regular, regular italic, semi bold,
semi bold italic, bold, bold italic,
black

abcdefghijklmnopqrstuvwxyz
ABCDEFGHIJKLMNOPQRSTUVWXYZ
1234567890 1234567890 &£$.,:;!?''

abcdefghijklmnopqrstuvwxyz
ABCDEFGHIJKLMNOPQRSTUVWXYZ
1234567890 1234567890 &£$.,:;!?''

Mirarae

Carol Twombly
Morisawa
1989

Bitstream

Regular, bold

Won an annual Morisawa type
design competition

abcdefghijklmnopqrstuvwxyz
ABCDEFGHIJKLMNOPQRSTUVWXYZ
1234567890 &£$.,:;!?''

abcdefghijklmnopqrstuvwxyz
ABCDEFGHIJKLMNOPQRSTUVWXYZ
1234567890 &£$.,:;!?''

ITC Mixage

Aldo Novarese
International Typeface Corporation
1985

Autologic, Berthold, Compugraphic,
Linotype, Scangraphic, Varityper
Humanist 785 (Bitstream)

Book, book italic, medium, medium
italic, bold, bold italic, black, black
italic

Designed originally for the Haas
typefoundry

abcdefghijklmnopqrstuvwxyz
ABCDEFGHIJKLMNOPQRSTUVWXYZ
1234567890 &£$.,:;!?''

abcdefghijklmnopqrstuvwxyz
ABCDEFGHIJKLMNOPQRSTUVWXYZ
1234567890 &£$.,:;!?''

abcdefghijklmnopqrstuvwxyz
ABCDEFGHIJKLMNOPQRSTUVWXYZ
1234567890 &£$.,:;!?''

abcdefghijklmnopqrstuvwxyz
ABCDEFGHIJKLMNOPQRSTUVWXYZ
1234567890 &£$.,:;!?''

Modern

Walter Tracy
Linotype
1969

Monotype

Medium, medium italic, bold

First used for *The Daily Telegraph* newspaper in London during May 1969. Known variously as Linotype Modern and Telegraph Modern. Released by Monotype as News Modern

abcdefghijklmnopqrstuvwxyz
ABCDEFGHIJKLMNOPQRSTUVWXYZ
1234567890 &£$.,:;!?''

abcdefghijklmnopqrstuvwxyz
ABCDEFGHIJKLMNOPQRSTUVWXYZ
1234567890 &£$.,:;!?''

ITC Modern 216

Edward Benguiat
International Typeface Corporation
1982

Autologic, Berthold, Compugraphic, Linotype, Scangraphic, Varityper

Light, light italic, medium, medium italic, bold, bold italic, heavy, heavy italic

abcdefghijklmnopqrstuvwxyz
ABCDEFGHIJKLMNOPQRSTUVWXYZ
1234567890 &£$.,:;!?''

abcdefghijklmnopqrstuvwxyz
ABCDEFGHIJKLMNOPQRSTUVWXYZ
1234567890 &£$.,:;!?''

abcdefghijklmnopqrstuvwxyz
ABCDEFGHIJKLMNOPQRSTUVWXYZ
1234567890 &£$.,:;!?''

abcdefghijklmnopqrstuvwxyz
ABCDEFGHIJKLMNOPQRSTUVWXYZ
1234567890 &£$.,:;!?''

Monanti

Erwin Koch
Hell
1977

Medium, semi bold

abcdefghijklmnopqrstuvwxyz
ABCDEFGHIJKLMNOPQRSTUVWXYZ
1234567890 &£$.,:;!?''

abcdefghijklmnopqrstuvwxyz
ABCDEFGHIJKLMNOPQRSTUVWXYZ
1234567890 &£$.,:;!?''

Monti

Erwin Koch
Hell
1989

Regular and semi bold

abcdefghijklmnopqrstuvwxyz
ABCDEFGHIJKLMNOPQRSTUVWXYZ
1234567890 &£$.,:;!?''

abcdefghijklmnopqrstuvwxyz
ABCDEFGHIJKLMNOPQRSTUVWXYZ
1234567890 &£$.,:;!?''

Napoleon

Wulf Jarosch
Hell
1976

Light, regular, regular italic, semi bold, bold, bold condensed, bold outline

abcdefghijklmnopqrstuvwxyz
ABCDEFGHIJKLMNOPQRSTUVWXYZ
1234567890 &£$.,:;!?"

abcdefghijklmnopqrstuvwxyz
ABCDEFGHIJKLMNOPQRSTUVWXYZ
1234567890 &£$.,:;!?"

abcdefghijklmnopqrstuvwxyz
ABCDEFGHIJKLMNOPQRSTUVWXYZ
1234567890 &£$.,:;!?"

abcdefghijklmnopqrstuvwxyz
ABCDEFGHIJKLMNOPQRSTUVWXYZ
1234567890 &£$.,:;!?"

Neue Helvetica

Staff designers
Linotype (Stempel)
1983

Geneva 2 (Autologic)
Helvetica No.2 (Berthold)
CG Triumvirate No.2
(Compugraphic)
HV (Itek)
Europa Grotesk No.2 (Scangraphic)

Ultra light extended, ultra light, ultra light italic, ultra light condensed, thin extended, thin, thin italic, thin condensed, light extended, light, light italic, light condensed, regular extended, regular, regular italic, regular condensed, medium extended, medium, medium italic, medium condensed, bold extended, bold, bold italic, bold condensed, heavy extended, heavy, heavy italic, heavy condensed, black extended, black, black italic, black condensed, bold outline, ultra black condensed

Re-working of the original Helvetica to satisfy current taste and to complement changes in technology

abcdefghijklmnopqrstuvwxyz
ABCDEFGHIJKLMNOPQRSTUVWXYZ
1234567890 &£$.,:;!?''

abcdefghijklmnopqrstuvwxyz
ABCDEFGHIJKLMNOPQRSTUVWXYZ
1234567890 &£$.,:;!?''

abcdefghijklmnopqrstuvwxyz
ABCDEFGHIJKLMNOPQRSTUVWXYZ
1234567890 &£$.,:;!?''

abcdefghijklmnopqrstuvwxyz
ABCDEFGHIJKLMNOPQRSTUVWXYZ
1234567890 &£$.,:;!?''

Neue Luthersche Fraktur

Volker Kuster
Scangraphic
1984

Regular, medium, headline

abcdefghijklmnopqrstuvwxyz
ABCDEFGHIJKLMNOPQRSTUVWXYZ
1234567890 &£$.,:;!?''

abcdefghijklmnopqrstuvwxyz
ABCDEFGHIJKLMNOPQRSTUVWXYZ
1234567890 &£$.,:;!?''

abcdefghijklmnopqrstuvwxyz
ABCDEFGHIJKLMNOPQRSTUVWXYZ
1234567890 &£$.,:;!?''

WTC Neufont

David Weinz
World Typeface Center
1987

Light, light italic, regular, regular italic, medium, medium italic, bold, bold italic

Re-working of Weinz Kurvalin (q.v.) released previously by Itek

abcdefghijklmnopqrstuvwxyz
ABCDEFGHIJKLMNOPQRSTUVWXYZ
1234567890 &$¢£:;!?

abcdefghijklmnopqrstuvwxyz
ABCDEFGHIJKLMNOPQRSTUVWXYZ
1234567890 &$¢£:;!?

abcdefghijklmnopqrstuvwxyz
ABCDEFGHIJKLMNOPQRSTUVWXYZ
1234567890 &$¢£:;!?

abcdefghijklmnopqrstuvwxyz
ABCDEFGHIJKLMNOPQRSTUVWXYZ
1234567890 &$¢£:;!?

Neuzeit S

Staff designers
Linotype (Stempel)
1966

Berthold, Monotype
Grotesk S (Scangraphic)

Book, book heavy

abcdefghijklmnopqrstuvwxyz
ABCDEFGHIJKLMNOPQRSTUVWXYZ
1234567890 &£$.,:;!?"

abcdefghijklmnopqrstuvwxyz
ABCDEFGHIJKLMNOPQRSTUVWXYZ
1234567890 &£$.,:;!?"

113

ITC New Baskerville

Staff designers
International Typeface Corporation
1982

Adobe, Autologic, Berthold,
Compugraphic, Hell, Linotype,
Monotype, Scangraphic, Varityper

Roman, italic, semi bold, semi bold
italic, book, book italic, black, black
italic

Freely adapted from the original
design of 1762 by John Baskerville:
the present version was developed
by Linotype in 1978 and made
available by licensing to ITC

abcdefghijklmnopqrstuvwxyz
ABCDEFGHIJKLMNOPQRSTUVWXYZ
1234567890 1234567890 &£$.,:;!?""

abcdefghijklmnopqrstuvwxyz
ABCDEFGHIJKLMNOPQRSTUVWXYZ
1234567890 &£$.,:;!?""

abcdefghijklmnopqrstuvwxyz
ABCDEFGHIJKLMNOPQRSTUVWXYZ
1234567890 &£$.,:;!?""

abcdefghijklmnopqrstuvwxyz
ABCDEFGHIJKLMNOPQRSTUVWXYZ
1234567890 &£$.,:;!?""

New Caledonia

Staff designers
Linotype (Mergenthaler)
1979

Adobe

Regular, regular italic, semi bold,
semi bold italic, bold, bold italic,
black, black italic

After Caledonia of 1938 by W A
Dwiggins

abcdefghijklmnopqrstuvwxyz
ABCDEFGHIJKLMNOPQRSTUVWXYZ
1234567890 1234567890 &£$.,:;!?""

abcdefghijklmnopqrstuvwxyz
ABCDEFGHIJKLMNOPQRSTUVWXYZ
1234567890 &£$.,:;!?""

abcdefghijklmnopqrstuvwxyz
ABCDEFGHIJKLMNOPQRSTUVWXYZ
1234567890 &£$.,:;!?""

abcdefghijklmnopqrstuvwxyz
ABCDEFGHIJKLMNOPQRSTUVWXYZ
1234567890 &£$.,:;!?""

ITC Newtext

Ray Baker
International Typeface Corporation
1974

Autologic, Berthold, Compugraphic,
Linotype, Monotype, Scangraphic,
Varityper
Copperplate 421 (Bitstream)
NT (Itek)

Light, light italic, book, book italic,
regular, regular italic, demi, demi
italic

abcdefghijklmnopqrstuvwxyz
ABCDEFGHIJKLMNOPQRSTUVWXYZ
1234567890 &£$.,:;!?"

abcdefghijklmnopqrstuvwxyz
ABCDEFGHIJKLMNOPQRSTUVWXYZ
1234567890 &£$.,:;!?"

abcdefghijklmnopqrstuvwxyz
ABCDEFGHIJKLMNOPQRSTUVWXYZ
1234567890 &£$.,:;!?"

abcdefghijklmnopqrstuvwxyz
ABCDEFGHIJKLMNOPQRSTUVWXYZ
1234567890 &£$.,:;!?"

Nimrod

Robin Nicholas
Monotype
1980

Regular, regular italic, bold, bold
italic

Special versions have been
proportioned and drawn for the
composition of small advertisements
and of headlines, as well as of
newspaper text. First used by the
Leicester Mercury newspaper in the
year of introduction

abcdefghijklmnopqrstuvwxyz
ABCDEFGHIJKLMNOPQRSTUVWXYZ
1234567890 .,:;!?"

abcdefghijklmnopqrstuvwxyz
ABCDEFGHIJKLMNOPQRSTUVWXYZ
1234567890 .,:;!?"

abcdefghijklmnopqrstuvwxyz
ABCDEFGHIJKLMNOPQRSTUVWXYZ
1234567890 .,:;!?"

abcdefghijklmnopqrstuvwxyz
ABCDEFGHIJKLMNOPQRSTUVWXYZ
1234567890 .,:;!?"

Nofret

Gudrun Zapf-von Hesse
Berthold
1986

Light, light italic, regular, regular
italic, medium, medium italic, bold,
bold italic

abcdefghijklmnopqrstuvwxyz
ABCDEFGHIJKLMNOPQRSTUVWXYZ
1234567890 1234567890 &£$.,:;!?"

abcdefghijklmnopqrstuvwxyz
ABCDEFGHIJKLMNOPQRSTUVWXYZ
1234567890 &£$.,:;!?"

abcdefghijklmnopqrstuvwxyz
ABCDEFGHIJKLMNOPQRSTUVWXYZ
1234567890 &£$.,:;!?"

abcdefghijklmnopqrstuvwxyz
ABCDEFGHIJKLMNOPQRSTUVWXYZ
1234567890 &£$.,:;!?"

Noris Script

Hermann Zapf
Linotype (Stempel)
1976

Norris Script (Autologic)
Gail Script (Varityper)

One weight only

Noris is the Latin name for
Nuremburg, the home town of the
designer

abcdefghijklmnopqrstuvwxyz
ABCDEFGHIJKLMNOPQRSTUVWXYZ
1234567890 &£$.,:;!?"

ITC Novarese

Aldo Novarese
International Typeface Corporation
1980

Autologic, Berthold, Compugraphic,
Linotype, Monotype, Scangraphic,
Varityper
Latin 671 (Bitstream)
NO (Itek)

Book, book italic, medium, medium
italic, bold, bold italic, ultra

Designed originally for the Haas
typefoundry

abcdefghijklmnopqrstuvwxyz
ABCDEFGHIJKLMNOPQRSTUVWXYZ
1234567890 &£$.,:;!?"

abcdefghijklmnopqrstuvwxyz
ABCDEFGHIJKLMNOPQRSTUVWXYZ
1234567890 &£$.,:;!?"

abcdefghijklmnopqrstuvwxyz
ABCDEFGHIJKLMNOPQRSTUVWXYZ
1234567890 &£$.,:;!?"

abcdefghijklmnopqrstuvwxyz
ABCDEFGHIJKLMNOPQRSTUVWXYZ
1234567890 &£$.,:;!?"

OCR A

Anonymous
Public Domain
1966

Adobe, Berthold, Bitstream, Hell,
Itek, Linotype, Monotype,
Scangraphic, Varityper

Adopted as the standard optical
character recognition fount by the
American National Standards
Institute. It was revised in 1977 to
embrace another eleven characters
to accord with the character set of
the USASCII code

ABCDEFGHIJKLMNOPQRSTUVWXYZ
1234567890 &'.¬:;'?"'

OCR B

Adrian Frutiger
Public Domain
1968

Adobe, Autologic, Berthold,
Bitstream, Hell, Linotype,
Monotype, Scangraphic, Varityper

Roman only

Designed to be read by optical
character recognition machines,
while remaining pleasant and
legible to humans. Developed as the
regional standard OCR typeface by
the European Computer
Manufacturers' Association. It was
updated and extended in 1971

abcdefghijklmnopqrstuvwxyz
ABCDEFGHIJKLMNOPQRSTUVWXYZ
1234567890 &£.,:;!?"'

117

Octavian

Will Carter and David Kindersley
Monotype
1961

Roman, italic

Adapted for phototypesetting in
1978

abcdefghijklmnopqrstuvwxyz
ABCDEFGHIJKLMNOPQRSTUVWXYZ
1234567890 .,:;!?''

abcdefghijklmnopqrstuvwxyz
ABCDEFGHIJKLMNOPQRSTUVWXYZ
1234567890 .,:;!?''

Olympian

Matthew Carter
Linotype (Mergenthaler)
1970

Medium, medium italic, bold, bold
italic

Designed for newspaper text
initially as unit-cut matrices for TTS
linecaster setting

abcdefghijklmnopqrstuvwxyz
ABCDEFGHIJKLMNOPQRSTUVWXYZ
1234567890 &£$.,:;!?''

abcdefghijklmnopqrstuvwxyz
ABCDEFGHIJKLMNOPQRSTUVWXYZ
1234567890 &£$.,:;!?''

abcdefghijklmnopqrstuvwxyz
ABCDEFGHIJKLMNOPQRSTUVWXYZ
1234567890 &£$.,:;!?''

abcdefghijklmnopqrstuvwxyz
ABCDEFGHIJKLMNOPQRSTUVWXYZ
1234567890 &£$.,:;!?''

Orion

Hermann Zapf
Linotype (Mergenthaler)
1974

Medium, medium italic

abcdefghijklmnopqrstuvwxyz
ABCDEFGHIJKLMNOPQRSTUVWXYZ
1234567890 &£$.,:;!?''

abcdefghijklmnopqrstuvwxyz
ABCDEFGHIJKLMNOPQRSTUVWXYZ
1234567890 &£$.,:;!?''

Osiris

Gustav Jaeger
Berthold
1984

Light, light italic, regular, regular italic, demi bold, demi bold italic, bold, bold italic

abcdefghijklmnopqrstuvwxyz
ABCDEFGHIJKLMNOPQRSTUVWXYZ
1234567890 &£$.,:;!?"

abcdefghijklmnopqrstuvwxyz
ABCDEFGHIJKLMNOPQRSTUVWXYZ
1234567890 &£$.,:;!?"

abcdefghijklmnopqrstuvwxyz
ABCDEFGHIJKLMNOPQRSTUVWXYZ
1234567890 &£$.,:;!?"

abcdefghijklmnopqrstuvwxyz
ABCDEFGHIJKLMNOPQRSTUVWXYZ
1234567890 &£$.,:;!?"

ITC Pacella

Vincent Pacella
International Typeface Corporation
1987

Autologic, Berthold, Compugraphic, Linotype, Monotype, Scangraphic, Varityper
PC (Itek)

Book, book italic, medium, medium italic, bold, bold italic, black, black italic

Second typeface designed for ITC by Vincent Pacella, a man responsible for the 'typographic engineering' of many letter designs in the ITC collection

abcdefghijklmnopqrstuvwxyz
ABCDEFGHIJKLMNOPQRSTUVWXYZ
1234567890 &£$.,:;!?"

abcdefghijklmnopqrstuvwxyz
ABCDEFGHIJKLMNOPQRSTUVWXYZ
1234567890 &£$.,:;!?"

abcdefghijklmnopqrstuvwxyz
ABCDEFGHIJKLMNOPQRSTUVWXYZ
1234567890 &£$.,:;!?"

abcdefghijklmnopqrstuvwxyz
ABCDEFGHIJKLMNOPQRSTUVWXYZ
1234567890 &£$.,:;!?"

For **WTC Our Bodoni** see Supplement   For **Oxford** see Supplement

ITC Panache

Edward Benguiat
International Typeface Corporation
1988

Autologic, Berthold, Compugraphic,
Linotype, Monotype, Scangraphic,
Varityper

Book, book italic, bold, bold italic,
black, black italic

abcdefghijklmnopqrstuvwxyz
ABCDEFGHIJKLMNOPQRSTUVWXYZ
1234567890 1234567890 &£$.,:;!?''

abcdefghijklmnopqrstuvwxyz
ABCDEFGHIJKLMNOPQRSTUVWXYZ
1234567890 1234567890 &£$.,:;!?''

abcdefghijklmnopqrstuvwxyz
ABCDEFGHIJKLMNOPQRSTUVWXYZ
1234567890 1234567890 &£$.,:;!?''

abcdefghijklmnopqrstuvwxyz
ABCDEFGHIJKLMNOPQRSTUVWXYZ
1234567890 1234567890 &£$.,:;!?''

PaulMark

John Schappler
Itek
1977

One weight only

Itek was first to release the typeface,
but ownership rights rest with the
designer

ABCDEFGHIJKLMNOPQRSTUVWXYZ
1234567890 &£$.,:;!?''

Permanent Headline

Staff designers
Ludwig & Mayer
1968

Berthold

Regular, regular italic, outline

abcdefghijklmnopqrstuvwxyz
ABCDEFGHIJKLMNOPQRSTUVWXYZ
1234567890 &£$..!?''

For **Pelican** see Supplement

Photina

José Mendoza y Almeida
Monotype
1971

Regular, italic, semi bold, semi bold italic, bold, bold italic, ultra bold, ultra bold italic

Third typeface introduced by Monotype specifically for phototypesetting

abcdefghijklmnopqrstuvwxyz
ABCDEFGHIJKLMNOPQRSTUVWXYZ
1234567890 .,:;!?''

abcdefghijklmnopqrstuvwxyz
ABCDEFGHIJKLMNOPQRSTUVWXYZ
1234567890 .,:;!?''

abcdefghijklmnopqrstuvwxyz
ABCDEFGHIJKLMNOPQRSTUVWXYZ
1234567890 .,:;!?"

abcdefghijklmnopqrstuvwxyz
ABCDEFGHIJKLMNOPQRSTUVWXYZ
1234567890 .,:;!?"

Pictor

Staff designers
Compugraphic
1984

Light, medium, bold

Part of the Novus collection with Draco (q.v.) and Vela (q.v.) and designed to complement electronic modulation of the letter forms. Based on Folkwang issued by Klingspor in 1949

abcdefghijklmnopqrstuvwxyz
ABCDEFGHIJKLMNOPQRSTUVWXYZ
1234567890(.,:;"?!)$%/&

abcdefghijklmnopqrstuvwxyz
ABCDEFGHIJKLMNOPQRSTUVWXYZ
1234567890(.,:;"?!)$%/&

abcdefghijklmnopqrstuvwxyz
ABCDEFGHIJKLMNOPQRSTUVW
XYZ 1234567890(.,:;"?!)$%/&

TC Pioneer

Tom Carnase and Ronne Bonder
International Typeface Corporation
1970

Autologic, Berthold, Compugraphic,
Hell
Decorated 081 (Bitstream)

Titling of a single weight

AABCDEFGHHIJJKKLLMMNNOPQQRRSSTTUV
UWXYYZ1234567890ÆŒ$.,tfllʒ''''''
--·()*§¢¼%//

Plaza

Alan Meeks
Letraset
1975

Hell

Medium, ultra, decorative, inline

AAABBCCDDEEFFGGHHHIJJKKKLMMNNOOPPP
QQRRSSTTUUVVWWXXYYZZ
1234567890 &?!£$.,::

AABBCCDDEEFFGGHHHIJJKKLLMMNN
OOPPQRRSSTTUUVVWWXXYYZZ
1234567890 &?!£$.,::

AABBCCDDEEFFGGHHHIJJKKLLMMNNOOPP
QQRRSSTTUUVVWWXXYYZZ
1234567890 &?!£$.,::

AABBCCDDEEFFGGHHHIJJKKLLMMNNO
PPQRRSSTTUUVVWWXXYYZZ
1234567890 &?!£$%.,::

Poell

Erwin Poell
Berthold
1972

Black, outline, medium outline,
shaded

Poell Black

Poell Medium Outline

Poell Outline

POELL SHADED

Adobe Ponderosa

Anonymous
Adobe
1990

One weight only

Based on an early American design
for wood letter

Poppl-Antiqua

Friedrich Poppl
Berthold
1967

Regular, medium, bold, bold
condensed, bold condensed italic

Friedrich Poppl signed an exclusive
contract with H Berthold AG in
1967. He died in 1982 having
created an impressive range of
typefaces. Poppl-Antiqua was the
first design to result from the
association. It appeared initially for
display purposes and emerged
much later for text applications

Poppl-Antiqua
Poppl-Antiqua
Poppl-Antiqua
Poppl-Antiqua
Poppl-Antiqua

Poppl-College

Friedrich Poppl
Berthold
1981

Regular, medium, bold

Poppl-College 2 contains many
swash letters

abcdefghijklmnopqrstuvwxyz
ABCDEFGHIJKLMNOPQRSTUVWXYZ
1234567890 &£$.,:;!?''

abcdefghijklmnopqrstuvwxyz
ABCDEFGHIJKLMNOPQRSTUVWXYZ
1234567890 &£$.,:;!?''

Poppl-Exquisit

Friedrich Poppl
Berthold
1970

Regular, medium

Second typeface of Friedrich Poppl
released by Berthold. Poppl-Exquisit
is also available as transfer lettering
and contains many swash letters

abcdefghijklmnopqrstuvwxyz
ABCDEFGHIJKLMNOPQRSTUVWXYZ
1234567890 &£$.,:;!?''

abcdefghijklmnopqrstuvwxyz
ABCDEFGHIJKLMNOPQRSTU
VWXYZ 1234567890 &£$.,:;!?''

Poppl-Laudatio

Friedrich Poppl
Berthold
1982

Light, light condensed, regular, regular italic, regular condensed, medium, medium italic, medium condensed, bold, bold italic, bold condensed

Last and largest typeface family to be completed by Friedrich Poppl

abcdefghijklmnopqrstuvwxyz
ABCDEFGHIJKLMNOPQRSTUVWXYZ
1234567890 &£$.,:;!?"

abcdefghijklmnopqrstuvwxyz
ABCDEFGHIJKLMNOPQRSTUVWXYZ
1234567890 &£$.,:;!?"

abcdefghijklmnopqrstuvwxyz
ABCDEFGHIJKLMNOPQRSTUVWXYZ
1234567890 &£$.,:;!?"

abcdefghijklmnopqrstuvwxyz
ABCDEFGHIJKLMNOPQRSTUVWXYZ
1234567890 &£$.,:;!?"

Poppl-Nero

Friedrich Poppl
Berthold
1982

Light, bold

POPPL NERO
POPPL NERO

Poppl-Pontifex

Friedrich Poppl
Berthold
1976

Power (Scangraphic)
Brunswick (Varityper)

Regular, regular italic, medium,
medium condensed, bold

First of the Friedrich Poppl designs
released by Berthold to achieve
notability and commercial success

abcdefghijklmnopqrstuvwxyz
ABCDEFGHIJKLMNOPQRSTUVWXYZ
1234567890 1234567890 &£$.,:;!?"

abcdefghijklmnopqrstuvwxyz
ABCDEFGHIJKLMNOPQRSTUVWXYZ
1234567890 &£$.,:;!?"

abcdefghijklmnopqrstuvwxyz
ABCDEFGHIJKLMNOPQRSTUVWXYZ
1234567890 &£$.,:;!?"

Poppl-Residenz

Friedrich Poppl
Berthold
1977

Light, regular

abcdefghijklmnopqrstuvwxyz
ABCDEFGHIJKLMNOP
QRSTUVWXYZ
1234567890 &£$.,:;!? ''

abcdefghijklmnopqrstuvwxyz
ABCDEFGHIJKLMNOP
QRSTUVWXYZ
1234567890 &£$.,:;!? ''

Praxis

Gerard Unger
Hell
1977

Light, medium, semi bold, bold, heavy

Sanserif complement to Demos (q.v.). Sloped versions of Praxis are produced by electronic slanting on the output machine or a genuine italic can be used known as Flora (q.v.)

abcdefghijklmnopqrstuvwxyz
ABCDEFGHIJKLMNOPQRSTUVWXYZ
1234567890 1234567890 &£$.,:;!?"

abcdefghijklmnopqrstuvwxyz
ABCDEFGHIJKLMNOPQRSTUVWXYZ
1234567890 1234567890 &£$.,:;!?"

abcdefghijklmnopqrstuvwxyz
ABCDEFGHIJKLMNOPQRSTUVWXYZ
1234567890 1234567890 &£$.,:;!?"

abcdefghijklmnopqrstuvwxyz
ABCDEFGHIJKLMNOPQRSTUVWXYZ
1234567890 1234567890 &£$.,:;!?"

Present

Friedrich Karl Sallwey
Linotype (Stempel)
1974

Adobe
Tracey Script (Varityper)

Regular and bold

abcdefghijklmnopqrstuvwxyz
ABCDEFGHIJKLMNOPQRSTUVWXYZ
1234567890 &£$.,:;!?"

abcdefghijklmnopqrstuvwxyz
ABCDEFGHIJKLMNOPQRSTUVWXYZ
1234567890 &£$.,:;!?"

PE Proforma

Petr van Blokland
Purup Electronics
1989

Book, book italic, bold, bold italic

Designed specially for the composition of forms

abcdefghijklmnopqrstuvwxyz
ABCDEFGHIJKLMNOPQRSTUVWXYZ
1234567890 1234567890 &£$.,:;!?"

abcdefghijklmnopqrstuvwxyz
ABCDEFGHIJKLMNOPQRSTUVWXYZ
1234567890 1234567890 &£$.,:;!?"

Proteus

Freda Sack
Letraset
1983

Varityper

Light, medium, bold, extra bold

abcdefghijklmnopqrstuvwxyz
ABCDEFGHIJKLMNOPQRSTUVWXYZ
1234567890 &?!£$.,;:

abcdefghijklmnopqrstuvwxyz
ABCDEFGHIJKLMNOPQRSTUVWXYZ
1234567890 &?!£$.,;:

abcdeffghhijkklmmnnopqrsttuvwxyz
ABCDEFGHIJKLMNOPQRSTUVWXYZ
1234567890 &?!£$.,;:

abcdefghijklmnopqrstuvwxyz
ABCDEFGHIJKLMNOPQRSTUVWXYZ
1234567890 &?!£$.,;:

Quadriga-Antiqua

Manfred Barz
Berthold
1979

Regular, regular italic, demi bold, bold, extra bold

Based on alphabets designed by Johan Michael Smit, a Dutchman commissioned by Frederick II in 1729 to establish a typefoundry in Berlin. Through a series of commercial acquisitions and amalgamations the typeface in question eventually devolved to the Federal Printing Office in West Germany

abcdefghijklmnopqrstuvwxyz
ABCDEFGHIJKLMNOPQRSTUVWXYZ
1234567890 1234567890 &£$.,:;!?"

abcdefghijklmnopqrstuvwxyz
ABCDEFGHIJKLMNOPQRSTUVWXYZ
1234567890 &£$.,:;!?"

abcdefghijklmnopqrstuvwxyz
ABCDEFGHIJKLMNOPQRSTUVWXYZ
1234567890 &£$.,:;!?"

Quay

David Quay
Letraset
1985

Varityper

Light, book, book italic, medium, bold

Derived from Forum Titling designed in 1911 by Frederic Goudy after lettering inscribed on the Arch of Titus in Rome

abcdefghijklmnopqrstuvwxyz
ABCDEFGHIJKLMNOPQRSTUVWXYZ
1234567890 &?!£$.,;:

abcdefghijklmnopqrstuvwxyz
ABCDEFGHIJKLMNOPQRSTUVWXYZ
1234567890 &!?£$.,;:

abcdefghijklmnopqrstuvwxyz
ABCDEFGHIJKLMNOPQRSTUVWXYZ
1234567890 &?!£$.,;:

abcdefghijklmnopqrstuvwxyz
ABCDEFGHIJKLMNOPQRSTUVWXYZ
1234567890 &?!£$.,;:

ITC Quorum

Ray Baker
International Typeface Corporation
1977

Autologic, Berthold, Compugraphic, Hell, Linotype, Monotype, Scangraphic, Varityper
Flareserif 851 (Bitstream)
QM (Itek)

Light, book, medium, bold, black

abcdefghijklmnopqrstuvwxyz
ABCDEFGHIJKLMNOPQRSTUVWXYZ
1234567890 &£$.,:;!?"

abcdefghijklmnopqrstuvwxyz
ABCDEFGHIJKLMNOPQRSTUVWXYZ
1234567890 &£$.,:;!?"

For **ITC Quay Sans** see Supplement

Rainbow Bass

Saul Bass
Linotype (Mergenthaler)
1982

One weight only

abcdefghijklmnopqrstuvwxyz
ABCDEFGHIJKLMNOPQRSTUVWXYZ
1234567890 &£$.,:;!?"

Renault

Wolff Olins
Renault
1978

Autologic, Berthold, Linotype,
Scangraphic, Varityper

Light, light italic, bold, bold italic

Light version developed through
interpolation by the Ikarus computer
program

abcdefghijklmnopqrstuvwxyz
ABCDEFGHIJKLMNOPQRSTUVWXYZ
1234567890 &£.,:;!?"

abcdefghijklmnopqrstuvwxyz
ABCDEFGHIJKLMNOPQRSTUVWXYZ
1234567890 &£.,:;!?"

abcdefghijklmnopqrstuvwxyz
ABCDEFGHIJKLMNOPQRSTUVWXYZ
1234567890 &£.,:;!?"

abcdefghijklmnopqrstuvwxyz
ABCDEFGHIJKLMNOPQRSTUVWXYZ
1234567890 &£.,:;!?"

Raleigh

Adrian Williams
Fonts/Ingrama SA
1977

Autologic, Compugraphic, Linotype,
Scangraphic, Varityper

Light, regular, regular italic,
medium, demi bold, bold, extra bold

Based on an original alphabet
commissioned by Cape & Co from
Carl Dair in 1967 and known as
Cartier (q.v.). Subsequently re-
drawn by David Anderson for
Typesettra and named Raleigh.
Adrian Williams, prompted by Paul
Benedict of Conways, developed the
design into a full type family

abcdefghijklmnopqrstuvwxyz
ABCDEFGHIJKLMNOPQRSTUVWXYZ
1234567890 &£$.,:;!?"

abcdefghijklmnopqrstuvwxyz
ABCDEFGHIJKLMNOPQRSTUVWXYZ
1234567890 &£$.,:;!?"

Revue

Colin Brignall
Letraset
1969

Adobe, Compugraphic, Hell,
Linotype, Varityper
Informal 870 (Bitstream)

Light, regular, medium, shadow

Compugraphic has developed more
variants of this design than any
other supplier

abcdefghijklmnopqrstuvwxyz
ABCDEFGHIiJKLMNOPQRSSTUVWXYZ
1234567890 &?!£$.,;:

RitaScript

John Schappler
Itek
1978

One weight only

Itek was first to release the typeface,
but ownership rights rest with the
designer

*abcdefghijklmnopqrstuvwxyz
ABCDEFGHIJKLMNOPQRSTUVWXYZ
1234567890 &£$.,:;!?"*

Romic

Colin Brignall
Letraset
1979

Berthold, Compugraphic, Hell,
Linotype, Scangraphic, Varityper

Light, light italic, medium, bold,
extra bold, outline

Serif dispositions have been
arranged to allow the close fitting of
characters in the modern idiom
without clashing

abcdefghijklmnopqrstuvwxyz
ABCDEFGHIJKLMNOPQRSTTUVWXYZ
1234567890 &?!£$.,;:

*abcdefghhijklmmnnopqrstuvwxyz
ABCDEFGHIJKLMNOPQRSTTUVWXYZ
1234567890 &?!£$.,;:*

abcdefghijklmnopqrstuvwxyz
ABCDEFGHIJKLMNOPQRSTTUVWXYZ
1234567890 &?!£$.,;:

**abcdefghijklmnopqrstuvwxyz
ABCDEFGHIJKLMNOPQRSTTUVWXYZ
1234567890 &?!£$.,;:**

Rotation

Arthur Ritzel
Linotype (Stempel)
1971

Rotieren (Autologic)

Medium, medium italic, bold

Arthur Ritzel was in charge of the
punchcutting department at
Stempel

abcdefghijklmnopqrstuvwxyz
ABCDEFGHIJKLMNOPQRSTUVWXYZ
1234567890 &£$.,:;!?''

abcdefghijklmnopqrstuvwxyz
ABCDEFGHIJKLMNOPQRSTUVWXYZ
1234567890 &£$.,:;!?''

abcdefghijklmnopqrstuvwxyz
ABCDEFGHIJKLMNOPQRSTUVWXYZ
1234567890 &£$.,:;!?''

Rotis Semi Sans

Otl Aicher
Compugraphic
1989

Light, light italic, regular, regular
italic, medium, bold

abcdefghijklmnopqrstuvwxyz
ABCDEFGHIJKLMNOPQRSTUVWXYZ
1234567890 &!?ß,.;:"

abcdefghijklmnopqrstuvwxyz
ABCDEFGHIJKLMNOPQRSTUVWXYZ
1234567890 &$£—-!?ß,.;:"

abcdefghijklmnopqrstuvwxyz
ABCDEFGHIJKLMNOPQRSTUVWXYZ
1234567890 &$£—-!?ß,.;:"

abcdefghijklmnopqrstuvwxyz
ABCDEFGHIJKLMNOPQRSTUVWXYZ
1234567890 &$£—-!?ß,.;:"

131

Rotis Serif

Otl Aicher
Compugraphic
1989

Regular, regular italic, medium

abcdefghijklmnopqrstuvwxyz
ABCDEFGHIJKLMNOPQRSTUVWXYZ
1234567890 &$£—-!?ß,.;:"

abcdefghijklmnopqrstuvwxyz
ABCDEFGHIJKLMNOPQRSTUVWXYZ
1234567890 &$£—-!?ß,.;:"

abcdefghijklmnopqrstuvwxyz
ABCDEFGHIJKLMNOPQRSTUVWXYZ
1234567890 &$£—-!?ß,.;:"

Rotis Semi Serif

Otl Aicher
Compugraphic
1989

Regular, medium

abcdefghijklmnopqrstuvwxyz
ABCDEFGHIJKLMNOPQRSTUVWXYZ
1234567890 &$£—-!?ß,.;:"

abcdefghijklmnopqrstuvwxyz
ABCDEFGHIJKLMNOPQRSTUVWXYZ
1234567890 &$£—-!?ß,.;:"

132

Sabon

Jan Tschichold
Linotype/Monotype/Stempel
1967

Adobe, Berthold
Sybil (Autologic)
Classical Garamond (Bitstream)
Symposia (Compugraphic)
September (Scangraphic)
Berner (Varityper)

Regular, italic, bold, bold italic

Produced at the instigation of a group of German master printers requiring a design that could be set by hand in foundry types and on linecasters and Monotype machines without perceptible differences on the page. John Dreyfus has described Sabon as the first 'harmonised' type for composing by disparate methods

abcdefghijklmnopqrstuvwxyz
ABCDEFGHIJKLMNOPQRSTUVWXYZ
1234567890 &£.,:;!?"

abcdefghijklmnopqrstuvwxyz
ABCDEFGHIJKLMNOPQRSTUVWXYZ
1234567890 &£.,:;!?"

abcdefghijklmnopqrstuvwxyz
ABCDEFGHIJKLMNOPQRSTUVWXYZ
1234567890 &£.,:;!?"

abcdefghijklmnopqrstuvwxyz
ABCDEFGHIJKLMNOPQRSTUVWXYZ
1234567890 &£.,:;!?"

Sayer Esprit

Manfred Sayer
Berthold
1984

Light, bold

abcdefghijklmnopqrstuvwxyz
ABCDEFGHIJKLMNOPQRSTUVWXYZ
1234567890 &£$.,:;!?"

abcdefghijklmnopqrstuvwxyz
ABCDEFGHIJKLMNOPQRSTUVWXYZ
1234567890 &£$.,:;!?"

PE Scherzo

Albert Boton
Purup Electronics
1990

Regular, regular italic, demi bold,
demi bold italic, bold, bold italic

abcdefghijklmnopqrstuvxyz
ABCDEFGHIJKLMNOPQRSTUVWXYZ
1234567890

Schneider-Antiqua

Werner Schneider
Berthold
1987

Light, light italic, regular, regular
italic, medium, medium italic, bold,
bold italic

abcdefghijklmnopqrstuvwxyz
ABCDEFGHIJKLMNOPQRSTUVWXYZ
1234567890

abcdefghijklmnopqrstuvwxyz
ABCDEFGHIJKLMNOPQRSTUVWXYZ
1234567890

abcdefghijklmnopqrstuvwxyz
ABCDEFGHIJKLMNOPQRSTUVWXYZ
1234567890

abcdefghijklmnopqrstuvwxyz
ABCDEFGHIJKLMNOPQRSTUVWXYZ
1234567890

Schuller

Manfred H Schuller
Berthold
1986

Regular, demi bold, bold

abcdefghijklmnopqrstuvwxyz
ABCDEFGHIJKLMNOPQRSTUVWXYZ
1234567890 &£$.,:;!?"

abcdefghijklmnopqrstuvwxyz
ABCDEFGHIJKLMNOPQRSTUVWXYZ
1234567890 &£$.,:;!?"

Seagull

Adrian Williams
Fonts/Ingrama SA
1978

Autologic, Linotype, Scangraphic
Calligraphic 750 (Bitstream)
Sandpiper (Varityper)

Light, medium, bold, black

Based on an original idea and rough
sketches by Bob McGrath for a
projected typeface to be called
Salient

abcdefghijklmnopqrstuvwxyz
ABCDEFGHIJKLMNOPQRSTUVWXYZ
1234567890 &£$.,:;!?''

abcdefghijklmnopqrstuvwxyz
ABCDEFGHIJKLMNOPQRSTUVWXYZ
1234567890 &£$.,:;!?''

Seneca

Gustav Jaeger
Berthold
1977

Light, light italic, regular, regular
italic, medium, bold, extra bold

abcdefghijklmnopqrstuvwxyz
ABCDEFGHIJKLMNOPQRSTUVWXYZ
1234567890 &£$.,:;!?''

abcdefghijklmnopqrstuvwxyz
ABCDEFGHIJKLMNOPQRSTUVWXYZ
1234567890 &£$.,:;!?''

abcdefghijklmnopqrstuvwxyz
ABCDEFGHIJKLMNOPQRSTUVWXYZ
1234567890 &£$.,:;!?''

Serifa

Adrian Frutiger
Bauer (Neufville)
1967

Adobe, Berthold, Compugraphic,
Linotype, Scangraphic
Seraphim (Autologic)
Swiss Slabserif 722 (Bitstream)
Seriverse (Varityper)

Thin, thin italic, light, light italic,
medium, medium italic, bold, black,
bold condensed

Frutiger has described this design
as Univers with serifs

abcdefghijklmnopqrstuvwxyz
ABCDEFGHIJKLMNOPQRSTUVWXYZ
1234567890 &£$.,:;!?''

abcdefghijklmnopqrstuvwxyz
ABCDEFGHIJKLMNOPQRSTUVWXYZ
1234567890 &£$.,:;!?''

abcdefghijklmnopqrstuvwxyz
ABCDEFGHIJKLMNOPQRSTUVWXYZ
1234567890 &£$.,:;!?''

ITC Serif Gothic

Herb Lubalin and Antonio DiSpigna
International Typeface Corporation
1974

Adobe, Autologic, Berthold,
Compugraphic, Hell, Linotype,
Monotype, Scangraphic, Varityper
Copperplate 701 (Bitstream)
SG (Itek)

Light, regular, bold, extra bold,
heavy, black

Regular and bold weights
introduced in 1972, the other styles
were added later by Antonio
DiSpigna

abcdefghijklmnopqrstuvwxyz
ABCDEFGHIJKLMNOPQRSTUVWXYZ
1234567890 &£$.,:;!?''

abcdefghijklmnopqrstuvwxyz
ABCDEFGHIJKLMNOPQRSTUVWXYZ
1234567890 &£$.,:;!?''

Shannon

Kris Holmes and Janice Prescott
Compugraphic
1982

Book, book italic, bold, bold italic,
extra bold, extra bold italic

abcdefghijklmnopqrstuvwxyz
ABCDEFGHIJKLMNOPQRSTUVWXYZ
1234567890 &$£—-!?ß,.;:''

abcdefghijklmnopqrstuvwxyz
ABCDEFGHIJKLMNOPQRSTUVWXYZ
1234567890 &$£—-!?ß,.;:''

**abcdefghijklmnopqrstuvwxyz
ABCDEFGHIJKLMNOPQRSTUVWXYZ
1234567890 &$£—-!?ß,.;:''**

Shelley Script

Matthew Carter
Linotype (Mergenthaler)
1972

Operinia (Autologic)
English 111 (Bitstream)

Allegro, Andante, Volante

abcdefghijklmnopqrstuvwxyz
ABCDEFGHIJKLMNOPQRSTU
VWXYZ 1234567890 &£$.,:;!?''

abcdefghijklmnopqrstuvwxyz
ABCDEFGHIJKLMNOPQRSTUVWXYZ
1234567890 &£$.,:;!?''

abcdefghijklmnopqrstuvwxyz
ABCDEFGHIJKLMNOPQRSTU
VWXYZ 1234567890 &£$.,:;!?''

Sierra

Kris Holmes
Hell
1989

Regular, regular italic, bold, bold italic

abcdefghijklmnopqrstuvwxyz
ABCDEFGHIJKLMNOPQRSTUVWXYZ
1234567890 1234567890 &£$.,:;!?"

abcdefghijklmnopqrstuvwxyz
ABCDEFGHIJKLMNOPQRSTUVWXYZ
1234567890 1234567890 &£$.,:;!?"

abcdefghijklmnopqrstuvwxyz
ABCDEFGHIJKLMNOPQRSTUVWXYZ
1234567890 1234567890 &£$.,:;!?"

abcdefghijklmnopqrstuvwxyz
ABCDEFGHIJKLMNOPQRSTUVWXYZ
1234567890 1234567890 &£$.,:;!?"

Signa

André Gürtler, Christian Mengelt, and Erich Gschwind
Autologic
1978

Regular, regular italic, regular condensed, medium, medium italic, medium condensed, bold, extra bold

Winner of a typeface design competition launched by BobstGraphic at the Congress of the Association Typographique Internationale in 1977

abcdefghijklmnopqrstuvwxyz
ABCDEFGHIJKLMNOPQRSTUVWXYZ
1234567890 &£$.,:;!?''

abcdefghijklmnopqrstuvwxyz
ABCDEFGHIJKLMNOPQRSTUVWXYZ
1234567890 &£$.,:;!?''

abcdefghijklmnopqrstuvwxyz
ABCDEFGHIJKLMNOPQRSTUVWXYZ
1234567890 &£$.,:;!?''

ITC Slimbach

Robert Slimbach
International Typeface Corporation
1987

Autologic, Berthold, Compugraphic,
Linotype, Monotype, Scangraphic,
Varityper
SL (Itek)

Book, book italic, medium, medium
italic, bold, bold italic, black, black
italic

abcdefghijklmnopqrstuvwxyz
ABCDEFGHIJKLMNOPQRSTUVWXYZ
1234567890 1234567890 &£$.,:;!?"

abcdefghijklmnopqrstuvwxyz
ABCDEFGHIJKLMNOPQRSTUVWXYZ
1234567890 1234567890 &£$.,:;!?"

abcdefghijklmnopqrstuvwxyz
ABCDEFGHIJKLMNOPQRSTUVWXYZ
1234567890 1234567890 &£$.,:;!?"

abcdefghijklmnopqrstuvwxyz
ABCDEFGHIJKLMNOPQRSTUVWXYZ
1234567890 1234567890 &£$.,:;!?"

Snell Roundhand

Matthew Carter
Linotype
1965

Engravers Roundhand (Autologic)
English 401 (Bitstream)
Signet Roundhand (Compugraphic)
RH (Itek)
Penman Script (Varityper)

Regular, bold, black

Based on the hand of Charles Snell,
an English writing master of the
seventeenth century

abcdefghijklmnopqrstuvwxyz
ABCDEFGHIJKLMNOPQRSTUVWXYZ
1234567890 &£$.,:;!?"

abcdefghijklmnopqrstuvwxyz
ABCDEFGHIJKLMNOPQRSTUVWXYZ
1234567890 &£$.,:;!?"

abcdefghijklmnopqrstuvwxyz
ABCDEFGHIJKLMNOPQRSTU
VWXYZ 1234567890 &£$.,:;!?"

ITC Souvenir

Edward Benguiat
International Typeface Corporation
1970

Adobe, Autologic, Berthold,
Compugraphic, Hell, Linotype,
Monotype, Scangraphic, Varityper
(ATF version)
Freeform 731 (Bitstream)
SV (Itek)

Light, light italic, medium, medium
italic, demi, demi italic, bold, bold
italic, bold outline

Based on Souvenir Light designed
by Morris Fuller Benton for the
American Type Founders Co in 1914

abcdefghijklmnopqrstuvwxyz
ABCDEFGHIJKLMNOPQRSTUVWXYZ
1234567890 &£$.,:;!?"

abcdefghijklmnopqrstuvwxyz
ABCDEFGHIJKLMNOPQRSTUVWXYZ
1234567890 &£$.,:;!?"

abcdefghijklmnopqrstuvwxyz
ABCDEFGHIJKLMNOPQRSTUVWXYZ
1234567890 &£$.,:;!?"

abcdefghijklmnopqrstuvwxyz
ABCDEFGHIJKLMNOPQRSTUVWXYZ
1234567890 &£$.,:;!?"

Souvenir Gothic

George Brian
TypeSpectra
1977

Autologic, Berthold, Compugraphic,
Linotype

Light, light italic, medium, medium
italic, demi bold, demi bold italic,
bold

First typeface produced by
TypeSpectra for text applications. It
was originally prepared for headline
use only

abcdefghijklmnopqrstuvwxyz
ABCDEFGHIJKLMNOPQRSTUVWXYZ
1234567890 &£.,:;!?"

abcdefghijklmnopqrstuvwxyz
ABCDEFGHIJKLMNOPQRSTUVWXYZ
1234567890 &£.,:;!?"

abcdefghijklmnopqrstuvwxyz
ABCDEFGHIJKLMNOPQRSTUVWXYZ
1234567890 &£.,:;!?"

abcdefghijklmnopqrstuvwxyz
ABCDEFGHIJKLMNOPQRSTUVWXYZ
1234567890 &£.,:;!?"

For **Stadia** see page 29

Stone Informal

Sumner Stone
Adobe
1987

Autologic, Berthold, Linotype, Monotype, Scangraphic, Varityper

Medium, medium italic, semi bold, semi bold italic, bold, bold italic

Designed to meet the requirements of low-resolution laser printing and to harmonise with Stone Sans and Stone Serif. Licensed to the International Typeface Corporation in 1988

abcdefghijklmnopqrstuvwxyz
ABCDEFGHIJKLMNOPQRSTUVWXYZ
1234567890 1234567890 &£$.,:;!?''

abcdefghijklmnopqrstuvwxyz
ABCDEFGHIJKLMNOPQRSTUVWXYZ
1234567890 1234567890 &£$.,:;!?''

abcdefghijklmnopqrstuvwxyz
ABCDEFGHIJKLMNOPQRSTUVWXYZ
1234567890 1234567890 &£$.,:;!?''

abcdefghijklmnopqrstuvwxyz
ABCDEFGHIJKLMNOPQRSTUVWXYZ
1234567890 1234567890 &£$.,:;!?''

Stone Sans

Sumner Stone
Adobe
1987

Autologic, Berthold, Linotype, Monotype, Scangraphic, Varityper

Medium, medium italic, semi bold, semi bold italic, bold, bold italic

Designed to meet the requirements of low-resolution laser printing and to harmonise with Stone Serif and Stone Informal. Licensed to the International Typeface Corporation in 1988

abcdefghijklmnopqrstuvwxyz
ABCDEFGHIJKLMNOPQRSTUVWXYZ
1234567890 1234567890 &£$.,:;!?''

abcdefghijklmnopqrstuvwxyz
ABCDEFGHIJKLMNOPQRSTUVWXYZ
1234567890 1234567890 &£$.,:;!?''

abcdefghijklmnopqrstuvwxyz
ABCDEFGHIJKLMNOPQRSTUVWXYZ
1234567890 1234567890 &£$.,:;!?''

abcdefghijklmnopqrstuvwxyz
ABCDEFGHIJKLMNOPQRSTUVWXYZ
1234567890 1234567890 &£$.,:;!?''

Stone Serif

Summer Stone
Adobe
1987

Autologic, Berthold, Linotype,
Monotype, Scangraphic, Varityper

Medium, medium italic, semi bold,
semi bold italic, bold, bold italic

Designed to meet the requirements
of low-resolution laser printing and
to harmonise with Stone Sans and
Stone Informal. Licensed to the
International Typeface Corporation
in 1988

abcdefghijklmnopqrstuvwxyz
ABCDEFGHIJKLMNOPQRSTUVWXYZ
1234567890 1234567890 &£$.,:;!?''

abcdefghijklmnopqrstuvwxyz
ABCDEFGHIJKLMNOPQRSTUVWXYZ
1234567890 1234567890 &£$.,:;!?''

abcdefghijklmnopqrstuvwxyz
ABCDEFGHIJKLMNOPQRSTUVWXYZ
1234567890 1234567890 &£$.,:;!?''

abcdefghijklmnopqrstuvwxyz
ABCDEFGHIJKLMNOPQRSTUVWXYZ
1234567890 1234567890 &£$.,:;!?''

Stratford

Freda Sack and Adrian Williams
Fonts/Ingrama SA
1978

Linotype, Scangraphic

Regular, regular italic, bold, black

abcdefghijklmnopqrstuvwxyz
ABCDEFGHIJKLMNOPQRSTUVWXYZ
1234567890 &£$.,:;!?''

abcdefghijklmnopqrstuvwxyz
ABCDEFGHIJKLMNOPQRSTUVWXYZ
1234567890 &£$.,:;!?''

abcdefghijklmnopqrstuvwxyz
ABCDEFGHIJKLMNOPQRSTUVWXYZ
1234567890 &£$.,:;!?''

Swift

Gerard Unger
Hell
1985

Scangraphic

Light, light italic, regular, regular italic, bold, bold italic, bold condensed, extra bold, extra bold italic

abcdefghijklmnopqrstuvwxyz
ABCDEFGHIJKLMNOPQRSTUVWXYZ
1234567890 1234567890 &£$.,:;!?"'

abcdefghijklmnopqrstuvwxyz
ABCDEFGHIJKLMNOPQRSTUVWXYZ
1234567890 1234567890 &£$.,:;!?"'

abcdefghijklmnopqrstuvwxyz
ABCDEFGHIJKLMNOPQRSTUVWXYZ
1234567890 1234567890 &£$.,:;!?"'

abcdefghijklmnopqrstuvwxyz
ABCDEFGHIJKLMNOPQRSTUVWXYZ
1234567890 1234567890 &£$.,:;!?"'

ITC Symbol

Aldo Novarese
International Typeface Corporation
1984

Autologic, Berthold, Compugraphic, Linotype, Monotype, Scangraphic, Varityper
Copperplate 721 (Bitstream)

Book, book italic, medium, medium italic, bold, bold italic, black, black italic

Third design by Aldo Novarese for ITC, the two earlier ones being ITC Novarese (q.v.) and ITC Fenice (q.v.)

abcdefghijklmnopqrstuvwxyz
ABCDEFGHIJKLMNOPQRSTUVWXYZ
1234567890 1234567890 &£$.,:;!?''

abcdefghijklmnopqrstuvwxyz
ABCDEFGHIJKLMNOPQRSTUVWXYZ
1234567890 1234567890 &£$.,:;!?''

abcdefghijklmnopqrstuvwxyz
ABCDEFGHIJKLMNOPQRSTUVWXYZ
1234567890 1234567890 &£$.,:;!?''

abcdefghijklmnopqrstuvwxyz
ABCDEFGHIJKLMNOPQRSTUVWXYZ
1234567890 1234567890 &£$.,:;!?''

Sympathie

Ferdinay Duman
Hell
1989

Regular, regular italic, semi bold, semi bold italic, bold, bold italic

abcdefghijklmnopqrstuvwxyz
ABCDEFGHIJKLMNOPQRSTUVWXYZ
1234567890 &£$.,:;!?"

abcdefghijklmnopqrstuvwxyz
ABCDEFGHIJKLMNOPQRSTUVWXYZ
1234567890 &£$.,:;!?"

abcdefghijklmnopqrstuvwxyz
ABCDEFGHIJKLMNOPQRSTUVWXYZ
1234567890 &£$.,:;!?"

abcdefghijklmnopqrstuvwxyz
ABCDEFGHIJKLMNOPQRSTUVWXYZ
1234567890 &£$.,:;!?"

Syntax

Hans E. Meier
Linotype (Stempel)
1968

Berthold
Synthesis (Autologic)
Symphony (Compugraphic)
SX (Itek)
Synchron (Scangraphic)
Cintal (Varityper)

Medium, medium italic, bold, black, ultra black

abcdefghijklmnopqrstuvwxyz
ABCDEFGHIJKLMNOPQRSTUVWXYZ
1234567890 &£$.,:;!?''

abcdefghijklmnopqrstuvwxyz
ABCDEFGHIJKLMNOPQRSTUVWXYZ
1234567890 &£$.,:;!?''

abcdefghijklmnopqrstuvwxyz
ABCDEFGHIJKLMNOPQRSTUVWXYZ
1234567890 &£$.,:;!?''

Adobe Tekton

David Siegel
Adobe
1990

Regular, regular oblique

Based on the hand lettering of Francis D K Ching, an architect practising in Seattle

abcdefghijklmnopqrstuvwxyz
ABCDEFGHIJKLMNOPQRSTUVWXYZ
1234567890 &£$.,:;!?"fifl

abcdefghijklmnopqrstuvwxyz
ABCDEFGHIJKLMNOPQRSTUVWXYZ
1234567890 &£$.,:;!?"fifl

WTC Thaddeus

Thaddeus Szumilas
World Typeface Center
1982

Linotype

Light, light italic, regular, regular italic, medium, medium italic, bold, bold italic

Third design issued by the World Typeface Center

abcdefghijklmnopqrstuvwxyz
ABCDEFGHIJKLMNOPQRSTUVWXYZ
1234567890 &£.,:;!?"

abcdefghijklmnopqrstuvwxyz
ABCDEFGHIJKLMNOPQRSTUVWXYZ
1234567890 &£.,:;!?"

abcdefghijklmnopqrstuvwxyz
ABCDEFGHIJKLMNOPQRSTUVWXYZ
1234567890 &£.,:;!?"

abcdefghijklmnopqrstuvwxyz
ABCDEFGHIJKLMNOPQRSTUVWXYZ
1234567890 &£.,:;!?"

145

Tiemann

Walter Tiemann/Adrian Frutiger
Linotype (Stempel)
1981

Light, medium

Based on Tiemann issued by the Klingspor typefoundry in 1923. Adapted for *Die Zeit* magazine

abcdefghijklmnopqrstuvwxyz
ABCDEFGHIJKLMNOPQRSTUVWXYZ
1234567890 &£$.,:;!?"

abcdefghijklmnopqrstuvwxyz
ABCDEFGHIJKLMNOPQRSTUVWXYZ
1234567890 &£$.,:;!?"

ITC Tiepolo

AlphaOmega Typography
International Typeface Corporation
1987

Autologic, Berthold, Compugraphic, Linotype, Monotype, Scangraphic, Varityper

Book, book italic, bold, bold italic, black, black italic

abcdefghijklmnopqrstuvwxyz
ABCDEFGHIJKLMNOPQRSTUVWXYZ
1234567890 1234567890 &£$.,:;!?"

abcdefghijklmnopqrstuvwxyz
ABCDEFGHIJKLMNOPQRSTUVWXYZ
1234567890 1234567890 &£$.,:;!?"

abcdefghijklmnopqrstuvwxyz
ABCDEFGHIJKLMNOPQRSTUVWXYZ
1234567890 1234567890 &£$.,:;!?"

abcdefghijklmnopqrstuvwxyz
ABCDEFGHIJKLMNOPQRSTUVWXYZ
1234567890 1234567890 &£$.,:;!?"

ITC Tiffany

Edward Benguiat
International Typeface Corporation
1974

Adobe, Autologic, Berthold,
Compugraphic, Hell, Linotype,
Monotype, Scangraphic, Varityper
Revival 831 (Bitstream)
TY (Itek)

Light, light italic, medium, medium
italic, demi, demi italic, heavy,
heavy italic

Italic styles were added to the
family in 1981. Tiffany is said to be
founded on two earlier designs,
namely Ronaldson and Caxton.
Ronaldson was cut by the
typefoundry of MacKellar, Smiths
and Jordan in 1884 with Caxton Old
Style No.2 being issued a couple of
decades later by the American Type
Founders Co

abcdefghijklmnopqrstuvwxyz
ABCDEFGHIJKLMNOPQRSTUVWXYZ
1234567890 &£$.,:;!?"

abcdefghijklmnopqrstuvwxyz
ABCDEFGHIJKLMNOPQRSTUVWXYZ
1234567890 &£$.,:;!?"

abcdefghijklmnopqrstuvwxyz
ABCDEFGHIJKLMNOPQRSTUVWXYZ
1234567890 &£$.,:;!?"

abcdefghijklmnopqrstuvwxyz
ABCDEFGHIJKLMNOPQRSTUVWXYZ
1234567890 &£$.,:;!?"

Times Europa

Walter Tracy
Linotype
1972

Medium, medium italic, bold, bold
italic

Designed for *The Times* newspaper
in London. First used for the edition
of 9 October 1972

abcdefghijklmnopqrstuvwxyz
ABCDEFGHIJKLMNOPQRSTUVWXYZ
1234567890 &£$.,:;!?"

abcdefghijklmnopqrstuvwxyz
ABCDEFGHIJKLMNOPQRSTUVWXYZ
1234567890 &£$.,:;!?"

abcdefghijklmnopqrstuvwxyz
ABCDEFGHIJKLMNOPQRSTUVWXYZ
1234567890 &£$.,:;!?"

abcdefghijklmnopqrstuvwxyz
ABCDEFGHIJKLMNOPQRSTUVWXYZ
1234567890 &£$.,:;!?"

Today Sans Serif

Volker Kuster
Scangraphic
1989

Extra light, extra light italic, extra light condensed, extra light condensed italic, extra light extended, extra light extended italic, light, light italic, light condensed, light condensed italic, light extra condensed, light extended, light extended italic, regular, regular italic, regular condensed, regular condensed italic, regular extra condensed, regular extended, regular extended italic, medium, medium italic, medium condensed, medium condensed italic, medium extra condensed, medium extended, medium extended italic, bold, bold italic, bold condensed, bold condensed italic, bold extended, bold extended italic, ultra, ultra italic, ultra extended, ultra extended italic, black extended, black extended italic

abcdefghijklmnopqrstuvwxyz
ABCDEFGHIJKLMNOPQRSTUVWXYZ
1234567890 &£$.,:;!?''

abcdefghijklmnopqrstuvwxyz
ABCDEFGHIJKLMNOPQRSTUVWXYZ
1234567890 &£$.,:;!?''

abcdefghijklmnopqrstuvwxyz
ABCDEFGHIJKLMNOPQRSTUVWXYZ
1234567890 &£$.,:;!?''

abcdefghijklmnopqrstuvwxyz
ABCDEFGHIJKLMNOPQRSTUVWXYZ
1234567890 &£$.,:;!?''

ITC Tom's Roman

Tom Carnase and Ronne Bonder
International Typeface Corporation
1970

Berthold, Compugraphic, Varityper
Revival 758 (Bitstream)

One weight only

abcdefgghijklmnopqrstuvwxyz
ABCDEFGHIJKKLMNOPQQRRSTUVWXYZ
1234567890 &£.,:;!?""

Adobe Trajan

Carol Twombly
Adobe
1989

Regular, bold

Based on the Trajan column inscription erected in Rome during the year AD 113

ABCDEFGHIJKLMNOPQRSTUVWXYZ
1234567890 &£$.,:;!?"

ABCDEFGHIJKLMNOPQRSTUVWXYZ
1234567890 &£$.,:;!?"

148

Traveller

John Peters
Monotype
1964

One weight only

Designed originally for the British
Railways Board

abcdefghijklmnopqrstuvwxyz
ABCDEFGHIJKLMNOPQRSTUVWXYZ&

Trieste

Adrian Williams
Fonts/Ingrama SA
1983

Scangraphic

Light, medium, medium italic, bold

Based on an original design by F W
Kleukens

abcdefghijklmnopqrstuvwxyz
ABCDEFGHJKLMNOPQRSTUVWXYZ
1234567890 &£$.,:;!?"

abcdefghijklmnopqrstuvwxyz
ABCDEFGHJKLMNOPQRSTUVWXYZ
1234567890 &£$.,:;!?"

abcdefghijklmnopqrstuvwxyz
ABCDEFGHJKLMNOPQRSTUVWXYZ
1234567890 &£$.,:;!?"

Trinité

Bram de Does
BobstGraphic/Autologic
1981

Roman condensed, roman wide,
italic, medium condensed, medium
wide, medium italic, bold

Short, normal, and long ascenders
and descenders are provided with a
standard x-height

abcdefghijklmnopqrstuvwxyz
ABCDEFGHIJKLMNOPQRSTUVWXYZ
12345678901 12345678901 £$%†&ß!¡?¿[]()§«»*:;'',.°

abcdefghijklmnopqrstuvwxyz
ABCDEFGHIJKLMNOPQRSTUVWXYZ
12345678901 12345678901 £$%†&ß!¡?¿[]()§«»*:;'',.°

abcdefghijklmnopqrstuvwxyz
ABCDEFGHIJKLMNOPQRSTUVWXYZ
12345678901 12345678901 £$%†&ß!¡?¿[]()§«»*:;'',.°

abcdefghijklmnopqrstuvwxyz
ABCDEFGHIJKLMNOPQRSTUVWXYZ
12345678901 12345678901 £$%†&ß!¡?¿[]()§«»*:;'',.°

abcdefghijklmnopqrstuvwxyz
ABCDEFGHIJKLMNOPQRSTUVWXYZ
12345678901 £$%†&ß!¡?¿[]()§«»*:;'',.°

abcdefghijklmnopqrstuvwxyz
ABCDEFGHIJKLMNOPQRSTUVWXYZ
12345678901 £$%†&ß!¡?¿[]()§«»*:;'',.°

**abcdefghijklmnopqrstuvwxyz
ABCDEFGHIJKLMNOPQRSTUVWXYZ
12345678901 12345678901 £$%†&ß!¡?¿[]()§«»*:;'',.°**

Uncle Sam

Staff designers
Compugraphic
1974

Regular, stars, stripes, open

Arguably the first original design
issued by Compugraphic

ABCDEFGHIJKLMNOPQRSTUVWXYZ
1234567890 &$£—–!?.,:;'"

ABCDEFGHIJKLMNOPQRSTUVWXYZ
1234567890 &$£—–!?.,:;'"

ABCDEFGHIJKLMNOPQRSTUVWXYZ
1234567890 &$£—–!?.,:;'"

Haas Unica

André Gürtler, Christian Mengelt, and Erich Gschwind
Haas
1980

Autologic, Linotype, Scangraphic

Light, light italic, regular, regular italic, medium, medium italic, bold, bold italic, black, black italic

Designed after a thorough analysis of the characteristics of three popular sanserif typefaces, namely Helvetica, Univers, and Akzidenz Grotesk

abcdefghijklmnopqrstuvwxyz
ABCDEFGHIJKLMNOPQRSTUVWXYZ
1234567890 &£$.,:;!?''

abcdefghijklmnopqrstuvwxyz
ABCDEFGHIJKLMNOPQRSTUVWXYZ
1234567890 &£$.,:;!?''

abcdefghijklmnopqrstuvwxyz
ABCDEFGHIJKLMNOPQRSTUVWXYZ
1234567890 &£$.,:;!?''

abcdefghijklmnopqrstuvwxyz
ABCDEFGHIJKLMNOPQRSTUVWXYZ
1234567890 &£$.,:;!?''

University

Mike Daines
Letraset
1972

Adobe, Autologic, Compugraphic, Linotype, Scangraphic, Varityper
Revival 851 (Bitstream)
UY (Itek)

Medium, medium italic, bold, display

Freda Sack drew the italic style

abcdefghijklmnopqrstuvwxyz
ABCDEFGHIJKLMNOPQRSTUVWXYZ
1234567890 &?!£$.,:

aaabcddeffgghhij jkkllmmnnop pqqrrssttuuvvwwxxyyzz
AABCDEFFGGHJHIJJKKLMMNNOPPQRRSSTTUUVVWWXXYYZ
1234567890 &?!£$.,:

abcdefghijklmnopqrstuvwxyz
ABCDEFGHIJKLMNOPQRSTUVWXYZ
1234567890 &?!£$.,:

abcdefghijklmnopqrstuvwxyz
ABCDEFGHIJKLMNOPQRSTUVWXYZ
1234567890 &?!£$.,:

ITC Usherwood

Leslie Usherwood
International Typeface Corporation
1984

Autologic, Berthold, Compugraphic,
Linotype, Scangraphic, Varityper

Book, book italic, medium, medium
italic, bold, bold italic, black, black
italic

Leslie Usherwood established
Typesettra in Toronto during 1968, a
graphic studio responsible for
several novel alphabets

abcdefghijklmnopqrstuvwxyz
ABCDEFGHIJKLMNOPQRSTUVWXYZ
1234567890 &£$.,:;!?"

abcdefghijklmnopqrstuvwxyz
ABCDEFGHIJKLMNOPQRSTUVWXYZ
1234567890 &£$.,:;!?"

abcdefghijklmnopqrstuvwxyz
ABCDEFGHIJKLMNOPQRSTUVWXYZ
1234567890 &£$.,:;!?"

abcdefghijklmnopqrstuvwxyz
ABCDEFGHIJKLMNOPQRSTUVWXYZ
1234567890 &£$.,:;!?"

Adobe Utopia

Robert Slimbach
Adobe
1989

Regular, regular italic, semi bold,
semi bold italic, bold, bold italic,
headline black, titling capitals

abcdefghijklmnopqrstuvwxyz
ABCDEFGHIJKLMNOPQRSTUVWXYZ
1234567890 1234567890 &£$.,:;!?"

abcdefghijklmnopqrstuvwxyz
ABCDEFGHIJKLMNOPQRSTUVWXYZ
1234567890 1234567890 &£$.,:;!?"

abcdefghijklmnopqrstuvwxyz
ABCDEFGHIJKLMNOPQRSTUVWXYZ
1234567890 1234567890 &£$.,:;!?"

abcdefghijklmnopqrstuvwxyz
ABCDEFGHIJKLMNOPQRSTUVWXYZ
1234567890 1234567890 &£$.,:;!?"

Vario

Hermann Zapf
Hell
1982

Scangraphic

Roman and italic

abcdefghijklmnopqrstuvwxyz
ABCDEFGHIJKLMNOPQRSTUVWXYZ
1234567890 &£$.,:;!?,'

abcdefghijklmnopqrstuvwxyz
ABCDEFGHIJKLMNOPQRSTUVWXYZ
1234567890 &£$.,:;!?,'

Vela

Barbara Gibb
Compugraphic
1984

Light, medium, bold

Part of the Novus collection with
Draco (q.v.) and Pictor (q.v.) and
designed to complement electronic
modulation of the letter forms

abcdefghijklmnopqrstuvwxyz
ABCDEFGHIJKLMNOPQRSTUVWXYZ
1234567890(.,:;"?!)$%/&

abcdefghijklmnopqrstuvwxyz
ABCDEFGHIJKLMNOPQRSTUVWXYZ
1234567890(.,:;"?!)$%/&

ITC Veljovic

Jovica Veljovic
International Typeface Corporation
1984

Autologic, Berthold, Compugraphic,
Linotype, Scangraphic, Varityper

Book, book italic, medium, medium
italic, bold, bold italic, black, black
italic

First typeface produced by Jovica
Veljovic, a Yugoslav designer.
Subsequent examples of his work
are to be seen elsewhere in this
book

abcdefghijklmnopqrstuvwxyz
ABCDEFGHIJKLMNOPQRSTUVWXYZ
1234567890 1234567890 &£$.,:;!?"

abcdefghijklmnopqrstuvwxyz
ABCDEFGHIJKLMNOPQRSTUVWXYZ
1234567890 1234567890 &£$.,:;!?"

abcdefghijklmnopqrstuvwxyz
ABCDEFGHIJKLMNOPQRSTUVWXYZ
1234567890 1234567890 &£$.,:;!?"

abcdefghijklmnopqrstuvwxyz
ABCDEFGHIJKLMNOPQRSTUVWXYZ
1234567890 1234567890 &£$.,:;!?"

Venture Script

Hermann Zapf
Linotype
1969

Ventura (Autologic)

One weight only

Based on the handwriting of the
designer

abcdefghijklmnopqrstuvwxyz
ABCDEFGHIJKLMNOPQRSTUVWXYZ
1234567890 &£$. ,.;!?"

WTC Veritas

Ronald Arnholm
World Typeface Center
1988

Light, light italic, regular, regular
italic, medium, medium italic, bold,
bold italic

abcdefghijklmnopqrstuvwxyz
ABCDEFGHIJKLMNOPQRSTUVWXYZ
1234567890 &£$.,-:;!?"

abcdefghijklmnopqrstuvwxyz
ABCDEFGHIJKLMNOPQRSTUVWXYZ
1234567890 &£$.,-:;!?"

abcdefghijklmnopqrstuvwxyz
ABCDEFGHIJKLMNOPQRSTUVWXYZ
1234567890 &£$.,-:;!?"

abcdefghijklmnopqrstuvwxyz
ABCDEFGHIJKLMNOPQRSTUVWXYZ
1234567890 &£$.,-:;!?"

For **Vergil** see Supplement

Versailles

Adrian Frutiger
Linotype (Stempel)
1982

Light, light italic, medium, medium italic, bold, bold italic, black, black italic

abcdefghijklmnopqrstuvwxyz
ABCDEFGHIJKLMNOPQRSTUVWXYZ
1234567890 1234567890 &£$.,:;!?''

*abcdefghijklmnopqrstuvwxyz
ABCDEFGHIJKLMNOPQRSTUVWXYZ
1234567890 1234567890 &£$.,:;!?''*

abcdefghijklmnopqrstuvwxyz
ABCDEFGHIJKLMNOPQRSTUVWXYZ
1234567890 1234567890 &£$.,:;!?''

*abcdefghijklmnopqrstuvwxyz
ABCDEFGHIJKLMNOPQRSTUVWXYZ
1234567890 1234567890 &£$.,:;!?''*

Video

Matthew Carter
Linotype
1977

Light, light oblique, medium, medium oblique, bold, bold oblique, black, black oblique

Based on CRT Gothic of 1974 by the same designer

abcdefghijklmnopqrstuvwxyz
ABCDEFGHIJKLMNOPQRSTUVWXYZ
1234567890 &£$.,:;!?''

*abcdefghijklmnopqrstuvwxyz
ABCDEFGHIJKLMNOPQRSTUVWXYZ
1234567890 &£$.,:;!?''*

abcdefghijklmnopqrstuvwxyz
ABCDEFGHIJKLMNOPQRSTUVWXYZ
1234567890 &£$.,:;!?''

*abcdefghijklmnopqrstuvwxyz
ABCDEFGHIJKLMNOPQRSTUVWXYZ
1234567890 &£$.,:;!?''*

For **Visigoth** see Supplement

Vladimir

Vladimir Andrich
Alphatype
1966

Regular, regular italic, bold, bold italic, regular condensed, bold condensed

abcdefghijklmnopqrstuvwxyz
ABCDEFGHIJKLMNOPQRSTUVWXYZ
1234567890 &£$.,:;!?''

abcdefghijklmnopqrstuvwxyz
ABCDEFGHIJKLMNOPQRSTUVWXYZ
1234567890 &£$.,:;!?''

abcdefghijklmnopqrstuvwxyz
ABCDEFGHIJKLMNOPQRSTUVWXYZ
1234567890 &£$.,:;!?''

abcdefghijklmnopqrstuvwxyz
ABCDEFGHIJKLMNOPQRSTUVWXYZ
1234567890 &£$.,:;!?''

Linotype Walbaum

Staff designers
Linotype
1960

Roman and italic

abcdefghijklmnopqrstuvwxyz
ABCDEFGHIJKLMNOPQRSTUVWXYZ
1234567890 1234567890 &£$.,:;!?''

abcdefghijklmnopqrstuvwxyz
ABCDEFGHIJKLMNOPQRSTUVWXYZ
1234567890 1234567890 &£$.,:;!?''

Walbaum Buch

Günter Gerhard Lange
Berthold
1975

Regular, regular italic, medium, medium italic, bold, bold italic

Berthold acquired the original Walbaum artefacts and archive material in 1919 and this version of the design is based on a 16-point hot-metal model

abcdefghijklmnopqrstuvwxyz
ABCDEFGHIJKLMNOPQRSTUVWXYZ
1234567890 1234567890 &£$.,:;!?"

abcdefghijklmnopqrstuvwxyz
ABCDEFGHIJKLMNOPQRSTUVWXYZ
1234567890 &£$.,:;!?"

abcdefghijklmnopqrstuvwxyz
ABCDEFGHIJKLMNOPQRSTUVWXYZ
1234567890 &£$.,:;!?"

abcdefghijklmnopqrstuvwxyz
ABCDEFGHIJKLMNOPQRSTUVWXYZ
1234567890 &£$.,:;!?"

Walbaum Standard

Günter Gerhard Lange
Berthold
1976

Regular, regular italic, medium

Based on 8- and 10-point specimens of a handcut original fount

abcdefghijklmnopqrstuvwxyz
ABCDEFGHIJKLMNOPQRSTUVWXYZ
1234567890 1234567890 &£$.,:;!?"

abcdefghijklmnopqrstuvwxyz
ABCDEFGHIJKLMNOPQRSTUVWXYZ
1234567890 &£$.,:;!?"

abcdefghijklmnopqrstuvwxyz
ABCDEFGHIJKLMNOPQRSTUVWXYZ
1234567890 &£$.,:;!?"

Washington

Russell Bean
Type Designers International
1970

Berthold

Extra light, light, regular, bold, black

Washington

Washington

Washington

Washington Black

ITC Weidemann

Kurt Weidemann
International Typeface Corporation
1983

Autologic, Berthold, Compugraphic, Linotype, Monotype, Scangraphic, Varityper

Book, book italic, medium, medium italic, bold, bold italic, black, black italic

Formerly known as Biblica, the face was commissioned by the German Bible Society for publication in 1982 of a translation jointly sponsored by the Catholic and Protestant church authorities. Kurt Strecker executed the master drawings after the design of Kurt Weidemann

abcdefghijklmnopqrstuvwxyz
ABCDEFGHIJKLMNOPQRSTUVWXYZ
1234567890 1234567890 &£$.,:;!?"

abcdefghijklmnopqrstuvwxyz
ABCDEFGHIJKLMNOPQRSTUVWXYZ
1234567890 1234567890 &£$.,:;!?"

abcdefghijklmnopqrstuvwxyz
ABCDEFGHIJKLMNOPQRSTUVWXYZ
1234567890 1234567890 &£$.,:;!?"

abcdefghijklmnopqrstuvwxyz
ABCDEFGHIJKLMNOPQRSTUVWXYZ
1234567890 1234567890 &£$.,:;!?"

Weinz Kurvalin

David Weinz
Itek
1982

Medium, medium italic, bold

Re-worked as Neufont (q.v.) and
issued by the World Typeface Center
in 1987

abcdefghijklmnopqrstuvwxyz
ABCDEFGHIJKLMNOPQRSTUVWXYZ
1234567890 &£$.,:;!?''

abcdefghijklmnopqrstuvwxyz
ABCDEFGHIJKLMNOPQRSTUVWXYZ
1234567890 &£$.,:;!?''

abcdefghijklmnopqrstuvwxyz
ABCDEFGHIJKLMNOPQRSTUVWXYZ
1234567890 &£$.,:;!?''

Wilke

Martin Wilke
Linotype
1988

Regular, regular italic, bold, bold
italic, black, black italic

abcdefghijklmnopqrstuvwxyz
ABCDEFGHIJKLMNOPQRSTUVWXYZ
1234567890 1234567890 &£$.,:;!?''

abcdefghijklmnopqrstuvwxyz
ABCDEFGHIJKLMNOPQRSTUVWXYZ
1234567890 1234567890 &£$.,:;!?''

abcdefghijklmnopqrstuvwxyz
ABCDEFGHIJKLMNOPQRSTUVWXYZ
1234567890 1234567890 &£$.,:;!?''

abcdefghijklmnopqrstuvwxyz
ABCDEFGHIJKLMNOPQRSTUVWXYZ
1234567890 1234567890 &£$.,:;!?''

For **Wile Roman** see Supplement

159

Woop De Doo Bold

Robert Stefanic
Varityper
1987

One weight only

Not dissimilar to the titling fount
Gold Nugget from Compugraphic

abcdefghijklmnopqrstuvwxyz
ABCDEFGHIJKLMNOPQRSTUVWXYZ
1234567890 &£$.,:;!?''

abcdefghijklmnopqrstuvwxyz
ABCDEFGHIJKLMNOPQRSTUVWXYZ
1234567890 &£$.,:;!?''

Worcester Round

Adrian Williams
Fonts/Ingrama SA
1974

Autologic, Linotype, Scangraphic

Regular, regular italic, medium,
bold, outline, rimmed (or
contoured), shaded

abcdefghijklmnopqrstuvwxyz
ABCDEFGHIJKLMNOPQRSTUVWXYZ
1234567890 &£$.,:;!?''

abcdefghijklmnopqrstuvwxyz
ABCDEFGHIJKLMNOPQRSTUVWXYZ
1234567890 &£$.,:;!?''

abcdefghijklmnopqrstuvwxyz
ABCDEFGHIJKLMNOPQRSTUVWXYZ
1234567890 &£$.,:;!?''

ITC Zapf Book

Hermann Zapf
International Typeface Corporation
1976

Autologic, Berthold, Compugraphic,
Hell, Linotype, Monotype,
Scangraphic, Varityper
Elliptical 716 (Bitstream)
ZF (Itek)

Light, light italic, medium, medium
italic, demi, demi italic, heavy,
heavy italic

Has a resemblance to the earlier
Hunt Roman of 1962 by the same
designer

abcdefghijklmnopqrstuvwxyz
ABCDEFGHIJKLMNOPQRSTUVWXYZ
1234567890 &£$.,:;!?''

abcdefghijklmnopqrstuvwxyz
ABCDEFGHIJKLMNOPQRSTUVWXYZ
1234567890 &£$.,:;!?''

abcdefghijklmnopqrstuvwxyz
ABCDEFGHIJKLMNOPQRSTUVWXYZ
1234567890 &£$.,:;!?''

abcdefghijklmnopqrstuvwxyz
ABCDEFGHIJKLMNOPQRSTUVWXYZ
1234567890 &£$.,:;!?''

ITC Zapf Chancery

Hermann Zapf
International Typeface Corporation
1979

Adobe, Autologic, Berthold,
Compugraphic, Hell, Linotype,
Monotype, Scangraphic, Varityper
Chancery 801 (Bitstream)
ZC (Itek)

Light, light italic, medium, medium
italic, demi, bold

Developed from an idea by Ed
Rondthaler for a broad-edged pen
Chancery script

abcdefghijklmnopqrstuvwxyz
ABCDEFGHIJKLMNOPQRSTUVWXYZ
1234567890 &£$.,:;!?''

abcdefghijklmnopqrstuvwxyz
ABCDEFGHIJKLMNOPQRSTUVWXYZ
1234567890 &£$.,:;!?''

abcdefghijklmnopqrstuvwxyz
ABCDEFGHIJKLMNOPQRSTUVWXYZ
1234567890 &£$.,:;!?''

ITC Zapf International

Hermann Zapf
International Typeface Corporation
1977

Autologic, Berthold, Compugraphic,
Hell, Linotype, Monotype,
Scangraphic, Varityper
Elliptical 717 (Bitstream)

Light, light italic, medium, medium
italic, demi, demi italic, heavy,
heavy italic

abcdefghijklmnopqrstuvwxyz
ABCDEFGHIJKLMNOPQRSTUVWXYZ
1234567890 &£$.,:;!?''

abcdefghijklmnopqrstuvwxyz
ABCDEFGHIJKLMNOPQRSTUVWXYZ
1234567890 &£$.,:;!?''

abcdefghijklmnopqrstuvwxyz
ABCDEFGHIJKLMNOPQRSTUVWXYZ
1234567890 &£$.,:;!?''

abcdefghijklmnopqrstuvwxyz
ABCDEFGHIJKLMNOPQRSTUVWXYZ
1234567890 &£$.,:;!?''

Zapf Renaissance

Hermann Zapf
Scangraphic
1987

Light, light italic, book, book italic,
bold

Fresh interpretation of Palatino, a
type family produced by the
designer in 1950. Work on Zapf
Renaissance began in 1984

abcdefghijklmnopqrstuvwxyz
ABCDEFGHIJKLMNOPQRSTUVWXYZ
1234567890 1234567890 &£$.,:;!?''

abcdefghijklmnopqrstuvwxyz
ABCDEFGHIJKLMNOPQRSTUVWXYZ
1234567890 1234567890 &£$.,:;!?''

abcdefghijklmnopqrstuvwxyz
ABCDEFGHIJKLMNOPQRSTUVWXYZ
1234567890 &£$.,:;!?''

Zipper

Staff designers
Letraset
1970

Hell

One weight only

abcdefghijklmnopqrstuvwxyz
ABCDEFGHIJKLMNOPQRSTUVWXYZ
1234567890 &?!€$.,;:

Agora

Albert Boton
Berthold
1990

Light, light italic, regular, regular
italic, medium, medium italic, bold,
bold italic

abcdefghijklmnopqrstuvwxyz
ABCDEFGHIJKLMNOPQRSTUVWXYZ
1234567890

abcdefghijklmnopqrstuvwxyz
ABCDEFGHIJKLMNOPQRSTUVWXYZ
1234567890

abcdefghijklmnopqrstuvwxyz
ABCDEFGHIJKLMNOPQRSTUVWXYZ
1234567890

abcdefghijklmnopqrstuvwxyz
ABCDEFGHIJKLMNOPQRSTUVWXYZ
1234567890

Amigo

Arthur Baker
AlphaOmega Typography
1989

Compugraphic

One weight only

Licensed exclusively to
Compugraphic

abcdefghijklmnopqrstuvwxyz
ABCDEFGHIJKLMNOPQRSTUVWXYZ
1234567890 &£$.,:;!?"

Arbiter

Aldo Novarese
Berthold
1989

Light, light italic, regular, regular
italic, medium, medium italic, bold,
bold italic

abcdefghijklmnopqrstuvwxyz
ABCDEFGHIJKLMNOPQRSTUVWXYZ
1234567890

abcdefghijklmnopqrstuvwxyz
ABCDEFGHIJKLMNOPQRSTUVWXYZ
1234567890

abcdefghijklmnopqrstuvwxyz
ABCDEFGHIJKLMNOPQRSTUVWXYZ
1234567890

abcdefghijklmnopqrstuvwxyz
ABCDEFGHIJKLMNOPQRSTUVWXYZ
1234567890

Avantis

Marco Ganz
Berthold
1988

Light, regular, medium, bold

abcdefghijklmnopqrstuvwxyz
ABCDEFGHIJKLMNOPQRSTUVWXYZ
1234567890 $£†&.,-;:!¡?*

abcdefghijklmnopqrstuvwxyz
ABCDEFGHIJKLMNOPQRSTUVWXYZ
1234567890 $£†*&.,-;:!¡?

Cornet

Gustav Jaeger
Berthold
1989

Light, light italic, regular, regular italic, medium, medium italic, bold, bold italic

abcdefghijklmnopqrstuvwxyz
ABCDEFGHIJKLMNOPQRSTUVWXYZ
1234567890

abcdefghijklmnopqrstuvwxyz
ABCDEFGHIJKLMNOPQRSTUVWXYZ
1234567890

abcdefghijklmnopqrstuvwxyz
ABCDEFGHIJKLMNOPQRSTUVWXYZ
1234567890

abcdefghijklmnopqrstuvwxyz
ABCDEFGHIJKLMNOPQRSTUVWXYZ
1234567890

Galathea

Hans Heitmann
Berthold
1990

Light, light italic, regular, regular italic, medium, medium italic, bold, bold italic

abcdefghijklmnopqrstuvwxyz
ABCDEFGHIJKLMNOPQRSTUVWXYZ
1234567890

abcdefghijklmnopqrstuvwxyz
ABCDEFGHIJKLMNOPQRSTUVWXYZ
1234567890

abcdefghijklmnopqrstuvwxyz
ABCDEFGHIJKLMNOPQRSTUVWXYZ
1234567890

abcdefghijklmnopqrstuvwxyz
ABCDEFGHIJKLMNOPQRSTUVWXYZ
1234567890

Helicon

David Quay
Berthold
1989

Light, light italic, regular, regular italic, medium, medium italic, bold, bold italic

abcdefghijklmnopqrstuvwxyz
ABCDEFGHIJKLMNOPQRSTUVWXYZ
1234567890

abcdefghijklmnopqrstuvwxyz
ABCDEFGHIJKLMNOPQRSTUVWXYZ
1234567890

abcdefghijklmnopqrstuvwxyz
ABCDEFGHIJKLMNOPQRSTUVWXYZ
1234567890

abcdefghijklmnopqrstuvwxyz
ABCDEFGHIJKLMNOPQRSTUVWXYZ
1234567890

Marigold

Arthur Baker
AlphaOmega Typography
1989

Compugraphic

One weight only

Licensed exclusively to Compugraphic

abcdefghijklmnopqrstuvwxyz
ABCDEFGHIJKLMNOPQRSTUVWXYZ
1234567890 &£$.,:;!?"

166

Mikaway

Kazimierz Mika
Berthold
1989

Light, light italic, regular, regular italic, medium, medium italic, bold, bold italic

abcdefghijklmnopqrstuvwxyz
ABCDEFGHIJKLMNOPQRSTUVWXYZ
1234567890

abcdefghijklmnopqrstuvwxyz
ABCDEFGHIJKLMNOPQRSTUVWXYZ
1234567890

abcdefghijklmnopqrstuvwxyz
ABCDEFGHIJKLMNOPQRSTUVWXYZ
1234567890

abcdefghijklmnopqrstuvwxyz
ABCDEFGHIJKLMNOPQRSTUVWXYZ
1234567890

Oxford

Arthur Baker
AlphaOmega Typography
1989

Compugraphic

One weight only

Licensed exclusively to
Compugraphic

abcdefghijklmnopqrstuvwxyz
ABCDEFGHIJKLMNOPQRSTUVWXYZ
1234567890 &£$.,:;!?"

Pelican

Arthur Baker
AlphaOmega Typography
1989

Compugraphic

One weight only

Licensed exclusively to
Compugraphic

abcdefghijklmnopqrstuvwxyz
ABCDEFGHIJKLMNOPQRSTUVWXYZ
1234567890 &£$.,:;!?"

ITC Quay Sans

David Quay
International Typeface Corporation
1990

Book, book italic, bold, bold italic,
black, black italic

abcdefghijklmnopqrstuvwxyz
ABCDEFGHIJKLMNOPQRSTUVWXYZ
1234567890 1234567890 &$¢£:;,.!?

Vergil

Dieter Hofrichter
Berthold
1990

Light, light italic, book, book italic,
medium, medium italic, bold, bold
italic

abcdefghijklmnopqrstuvwxyz
ABCDEFGHIJKLMNOPQRSTUVWXYZ
1234567890

abcdefghijklmnopqrstuvwxyz
ABCDEFGHIJKLMNOPQRSTUVWXYZ
1234567890

abcdefghijklmnopqrstuvwxyz
ABCDEFGHIJKLMNOPQRSTUVWXYZ
1234567890

abcdefghijklmnopqrstuvwxyz
ABCDEFGHIJKLMNOPQRSTUVWXYZ
1234567890

Visigoth

Arthur Baker
AlphaOmega Typography
1988

Compugraphic

One weight only

Designed for setting the text of
A Dante Bestiary published by
Ombondi Editions in New York
during 1989. Exclusively licensed to
Compugraphic

abcdefghijklmnopqrstuvwxyz
ABCDEFGHIJKLMNOPQRSTUVWXYZ
1234567890 &£$.,:;!?"

Wile Roman

Cynthia Hollandsworth
AlphaOmega Typography
1990

Compugraphic

Book, book italic, medium, medium
italic, bold, bold italic, black, black
italic

Licensed exclusively to
Compugraphic

abcdefghijklmnopqrstuvwxyz
ABCDEFGHIJKLMNOPQRSTUVWXYZ
1234567890 &£$.,:;!?''

abcdefghijklmnopqrstuvwxyz
ABCDEFGHIJKLMNOPQRSTUVWXYZ
1234567890 &£$.,:;!?''

abcdefghijklmnopqrstuvwxyz
ABCDEFGHIJKLMNOPQRSTUVWXYZ
1234567890 &£$.,:;!?''

abcdefghijklmnopqrstuvwxyz
ABCDEFGHIJKLMNOPQRSTUVWXYZ
1234567890 &£$.,:;!?''

WTC Our Bodoni

Massimo Vignelli and Tom Carnase
World Typeface Center
1989

Light, light italic, regular, regular
italic, medium, medium italic, bold,
bold italic

abcdefghijklmnopqrstuvwxyz
ABCDEFGHIJKLMNOPQRSTUVWXYZ
1234567890 &£$.,-:;!?''

abcdefghijklmnopqrstuvwxyz
ABCDEFGHIJKLMNOPQRSTUVWXYZ
1234567890 &£$.,-:;!?''

abcdefghijklmnopqrstuvwxyz
ABCDEFGHIJKLMNOPQRSTUVWXYZ
1234567890 &£$.,-:;!?''

abcdefghijklmnopqrstuvwxyz
ABCDEFGHIJKLMNOPQRSTUVWXYZ
1234567890 &£$.,-:;!?''

Some designer profiles

Otl Aicher

Born 1922 in Ulm. Studied sculpture at the Munich Academy of Fine Arts. Opened advertising design studio 1948. Developed corporate images for a number of major enterprises: Braun of Frankfurt (1954), Deutsche Lufthansa (1960), Olympic Games (1972), ZDF television network (1974), ERCO (1976), and the Berlin publishers Severin and Siedler (1980). Designed countless books and magazines, including *Lufthansa's Germany* in the latter category. Created signs for the Munich public transport system and airport and for Frankfurt airport. Has written several books on design theory: *The Kitchen's for Cooking* (1982) and *Critique of the Automobile* (1984).

Edward Benguiat

American designer of over 500 typefaces. Attended the Workshop School of Advertising Art and studied calligraphy under Arnold Bank and Paul Standard. Became Associate Director of *Esquire* magazine in 1953, followed by a spell of running his own design studio. Joined Photo-Lettering Inc in 1962 and continues with the company as Typographic Design Director. Served as vice-president of the International Typeface Corporation (ITC) and together with Herb Lubalin did much to develop the distinctive character of the *U&lc* magazine. His attributes include nine type families for ITC, as well as logotypes for the *New York Times*, *Playboy*, *Reader's Digest*, *Sports Illustrated*, *Esquire*, *Photoplay*, and *Look*. Professional affiliations encompass the New York Art Directors Club, the Type Directors Club, and the Alliance Graphique Internationale.

Charles Bigelow

Graduate of Reed College. Studied graphic arts, vision research, linguistics, and computer science at the San Francisco Art Institute, Portland State University, Rochester Institute of Technology, and Harvard University. Associate professor of typographic design at Rhode Island School of Design. Typographic adviser to Dr-Ing Rudolf Hell GmbH. Partner in Bigelow & Holmes, a studio located at Menlo Park, California specialising in letterform research and design. Associate editor of *Fine Print*, a journal dedicated to the arts of the book. In addition to work shown in this book, Charles Bigelow has collaborated with Kris Holmes to produce Leviathan for Berthold, Pellucida for video displays, and Syntax Phonetic, the latter in conjunction with Hans Meier for adapting the Syntax type (q.v.) to render the American Indian languages.

Constance Blanchard

Born in 1954 in Athol, Massachusetts. Studied at the University of Vermont and at the Massachusetts College of Art. Practised as a typographic artist and as Manager of Type Design for the Compugraphic Corporation.

Chris Brand

Born 1921 in Utrecht. Studied calligraphy in 1940. Worked in Brussels from 1948 to 1953. Taught type design and typography in various academies up to 1986. Designed numerous book covers and jackets, as well as several typefaces, lettering, a title line for a national newspaper, and a Hebrew fount.

Colin Brignall

Born 1940 in Warwickshire. Early career in press, fashion, and commercial photography. Joined Letraset 1964 as a photographic technician in the type studio. No formal training in typography, but benefited from studio practice and close supervision to develop distinctive letter design skills. Appointed Type Director for Letraset in 1980. Apart from the five type families for phototypesetting shown in this book, Colin Brignall conceived many typefaces for transfer lettering, exemplified by: Premier Lightline (1969), Premier Shaded (1970), Octopuss (1970), Superstar (1970), and Harlow (1977).

Margaret Calvert

Born 1936 in South Africa. Came to London in 1950 and attended St Paul's School. From 1954 to 1957 studied illustration at the Chelsea School of Art where the lecturers included Jock Kinneir, Hans Schleger, and Brian Robb. Started work in 1978 as an assistant to Jock Kinneir designing signs for Gatwick Airport and went to typography classes in the evening at the Central School of Art and Design. In 1964 became a partner in the design practice of Kinneir Calvert & Associates. Earned the Silver Award of the Design & Art Directors Association for outstanding book typography in 1978. Served as a part-time tutor at the Royal College of Art. Elected member of the Alliance Graphique Internationale in 1977.

Tom Carnase

Born 1939. Began career in the design division of Sudler & Hennessey Inc and stayed with the company for five years. Turned freelance and started own studio in 1964. Became vice-president of Lubalin, Smith, Carnase Inc in 1969. Returned to freelance work in 1979. Jointly founded the World Typeface Center Inc in 1980: an independent agency creating and licensing type designs to equipment manufacturers (similar to ITC) and issuing a house magazine called *Ligature*. Carnase Typography is another commercial interest of the designer. More than 50 alphabets have been designed by Tom Carnase. His other design work includes packaging, exhibitions, editorial design, corporate identities, and a host of logotypes exemplified by those for *New York* and *Esquire* magazines.

Ron Carpenter

Born 1950. Trained from 1968 as a letter draughtsman in the type drawing office of the Monotype Corporation and progressed to a typeface designer in 1982. Assisted Robin Nicholas in the design of Nimrod italic, as well as producing the families of Cantoria and Calisto shown in this book.

Matthew Carter

Born 1937. Trained as punchcutter and typefounder with the graphic arts group of Joh Enschedé en Zonen in the Netherlands. Cut replacement punches for the collection of Fell types at the Oxford University Press. Freelance designer 1957-63. Typographic adviser 1963-65 to Crosfield Electronics Ltd, designing characters for Photon phototypesetting machines. Staff designer with the American arm of the Linotype organisation 1965-71. Freelance designer in London 1971, continuing work for Linotype. Co-founder of Bitstream Inc in 1981, an independent producer and supplier of digital type based in Cambridge, Massachusetts. Typographic adviser to Her Majesty's Stationery Office 1980-84. Elected Royal Designer for Industry by the Royal Society of Arts in 1981.

Will Carter

Born 1912. Discovered printing as a hobby at the age of twelve after a visit to the Clarendon Press in Oxford and a gift of type from John Johnson, the printer. Trained in all aspects of printing at Unwin Brothers, Woking 1930-32. Commenced working in 1934 for Simon Shand in Hertford at an enterprise that later became the Shenval Press. Moved on briefly to employment with two advertising agencies in London and then went to Heffers printing house in Cambridge. Studied letter-cutting under David Kindersley 1948. Established the Rampant Lions Press in Cambridge 1949. Designed Klang typeface released by Monotype in 1955.

Antonio DiSpigna

Born 1943 in Italy. Emigrated with family to the USA and studied at the New York City Community College and Pratt Institute. Gained first design job in the studio of Bonder & Carnase Inc. and in 1969 joined Lubalin Smith Carnase Inc. Opened own design office in 1973. Later became a partner in Herb Lubalin Associates Inc. Resumed independent activities as Tony DiSpigna Inc. Teaches graduate courses in typography at Pratt Institute, School of Visual Arts, and the New York Institute of Technology.

Dick Dooijes
Born 1909 in the Netherlands. Joined the Amsterdam Typefoundry on leaving school and worked with S H de Roos (1877-1962). Studied at the Amsterdam College of Arts and Crafts and at the Academy of Art. His typefaces include Mercator (1958), Contura (1966), and Lectura (1969).

Roger Excoffon
Born 1910 in Marseilles. Read law at the University of Aix-en-Provence and later went to Paris in order to pursue the study of painting. Formed the U & O advertising agency in 1947 and became art director of the Fonderie Olive. Designed many typefaces, in addition to Antique Olive shown in this book, including Chambord (1945), Banco (1951), and Calypso (1958), and favoured the script form as evidenced by Mistral (1953), Choc (1955), and Diane (1956). Died 1983.

Ernst Friz
Born 1932 in Zurich. Studied at the Kunstgewerbeschule in his home town under Rudolf Bircher and Walter Kach: the latter also instructed Adrian Frutiger. Established own graphic art studio in Zurich specialising in typography, symbol and logotype creation, and packaging design. Won the Swiss national packaging award in 1962.

Adrian Frutiger
Born 1928 at Interlaken, Switzerland. Apprentice compositor at Otto Schlaefli AG. Studied at Kunstgewerbeschule in Zurich 1949-50. Appointed artistic director of Deberny & Peignot in Paris 1952. Designed several typefaces (prior to the period covered by this book) for the French typefoundry, instanced by President (1952), Phoebus (1953), Ondine (1953), Meridien (1954), and Univers (1954). Established own studio in 1962 with André Gürtler and Bruno Pfaffli. Designed Egyptienne for the Photon/Lumitype machine 1960; an early foray into phototypesetting. Art director for Editions Hermann, Paris 1957 to 1967. Engaged as typographic consultant for strike-on composition by IBM in 1963. Typographic adviser to the Linotype Group.

Karl Gerstner
Born 1930. Trained under Armin Hofmann and Emil Ruder at the School of Design in Basle. Co-founder of the advertising agency GCK which has been responsible for a number of promotional campaigns and corporate identities. Awarded in 1955 the gold medal of the Triennale de Milano for re-design of the journal *Werk*. Worked internationally as a designer of print media on *Capital*, *Test*, and *France Soir*. Written extensively on graphic design: *Integral Typography* (1959), *The New Graphic Art* (1959), *Designing Programs* (1963), and *Compendium for Literates* (1970). Entire issue of *Typografische Monatsblätter* dedicated to his work in 1972. Commissioned by Berthold to develop the venerable Akzidenz-Grotesk type design into an extensive and self-contained family in 1962. Undertaken work for IBM, including design of a Bodoni Manual.

Barbara Gibb
Born 1958 in Brighton, Massachusetts. Studied at the Southeastern Massachusetts University and obtained a Bachelor of Fine Arts degree in 1980. Practised as a type-lettering artist and became Supervisor of the New Type Design Department for the Compugraphic Corporation.

André Gürtler
Born 1936 in Switzerland. Studied typographic design. Worked consecutively in the type drawing office of the Monotype Corporation in England and of the Deberny & Peignot typefoundry

in France. Joined the studio of Adrian Frutiger and tutored in letterforms at the Académie Populaire des Arts Plastiques in Paris. Since 1965 has lectured on the history and design of letterforms at the School of Design, Basle. Attended as visiting lecturer at Yale University and at Universidad Autonoma Metropolitana in Mexico City. Partner in Team 77 with Erich Gschwind and Christian Mengelt, dealing in the entire field of lettering. Member of the editorial panel of *Typographische Monatsblätter* and contributed many articles to the magazine. Responsible for the Compugraphic version of Univers.

Cynthia Hollandsworth

American designer. President of AlphaOmega Typography Inc, a design studio specialising in typeface projects. Formerly associated with High Technology Solutions as Director of Typeface Development. Adviser to the Board of the International Typeface Corporation. Currently head of the Type Division for the Compugraphic Corporation.

Kris Holmes

Born 1950 in California. Learned calligraphy from Lloyd Reynolds and Robert Palladino at Reed College in Oregon. Later studied modern dance at the Martha Graham School in New York. Gained a Bachelor of Liberal Arts degree in Extension Studies from Harvard University. Designed several types for the firm of Dr-Ing Rudolf Hell, including revivals of Baskerville and Caslon in addition to those shown in this book. With Charles Bigelow created Lucida, the first original type family for low-resolution laser printing. Drew a new typeface for the re-design of *Scientific American* magazine. Her lettering and calligraphy have appeared in several publications, such as: *Fine Print*, *International Calligraphy Today*, *Publish!*, and *Scriptura '84*. She is a partner in Bigelow & Holmes.

Gustav Jaeger

Born 1925, the son of a printer. Studied at the Offenbach Art School and gained initial employment at the Bauer foundry developing type specimens and advising on the application of type designs. Several Berthold headlining founts are attributable to him, including Jumbo (1973), Komet (1976), Pinnochio (1973), and Semin-Antiqua (1976). His later work has encompassed text faces, exemplified by Daily News (1985), Jaeger-Antiqua (1984), Jersey (1985), and Seneca (1977).

Mark Jamra

Born 1956 in the USA. Began by studying architecture at college, but ended up with a degree in graphic design. Practised commercially as a designer, before undertaking postgraduate work at the Kunstgewerbeschule in Basle. Moved to Hamburg and joined URW, the developer of the Ikarus system for the digitisation of typefaces. Currently runs own design studio in the Hamburg area.

David Kindersley

Born 1915 at Codicote, Hertfordshire. Attended Marlborough College. Trained under Gilbert Ledward RA and apprenticed to Eric Gill at Pigotts 1934-36. Accomplished stone carver and lettering designer. Examples of work abound in war memorials (*eg* Trinity College, Cambridge), in Cambridge street names, in bookplates (*eg* Eric Gill Collection), in heraldic carving (*eg* Pembroke College, Cambridge), in portraits (*eg* Dr John Edward Goodwin, UCLA), in wood carving and engraving (*eg* Peterborough Cathedral). Chairman of the Wynkyn de Worde Society 1976. Much recent effort has been expended on the automatic optical spacing of capital letters by a computer program known as Logos from Cambridge SuperVision Ltd. In addition to the two typefaces shown in this book, David Kindersley has produced two titlings for the printing house W S Cowell Ltd in Ipswich, namely Scintilla and Tarquinius.

Volker Kuster

Born 1941 in Wernigerode, East Germany. Apprenticed as a typesetter. Attended the Arts Trade School in Berlin specialising in typography and graphic design from 1961 to 1964. Continued studies at Leipzig University in the book design department with Professor Albert Kapr. Went on to serve as tutor in typography and type design from 1969 to 1975 at the University of Leipzig. Over this period, Volker Kuster also undertook freelance design work in Leipzig and collaborated technically with Typoart in Dresden. Appointed Type Director for Scangraphic in Hamburg from 1984 to 1988. Gained two professorships in 1988 and 1989 respectively, in Hamburg and Essen, both concerned principally with typography and type design.

Günter Gerhard Lange

Born 1921 in Frankfurt. Studied at the Academy for the Graphic Arts and Book Production in Leipzig between 1941 and 1945. His tutors included Georg Belwe for calligraphy and typesetting and Hans Theo Richter for lithography. Later assisted Walter Tiemann at the same institution as a teacher. From 1945 to 1949 served as a freelance typographer and graphic artist. Moved to Berlin in 1949 to further studies at the University of Pictorial Arts. In 1950 started freelance work for H Berthold AG which was to blossom into a much more permanent and fruitful relationship. Between 1955 and 1960 taught typography at the School for Graphics and Book Production in Berlin. Appointed Artistic Director for H Berthold AG in 1961 and elected to the main Board of the company in 1971. Visited several academies as a guest lecturer in Kassel, Amsterdam, Munich, and other places. Received countless industrial honours. Designer of many type families, including Concorde and Imago.

Richard Lawrie

Born 1949. Trained at the Art Institute of Boston, Massachusetts. Held several positions in type design with the Compugraphic Corporation, Itek Composition Systems, and the Digital Equipment Corporation.

Joffre Lefevre

Born 1945 in Muskegon, Michigan. Studied at the Grandvalley State University and at the Kendall School of Design. Practised as a senior type lettering artist for the Compugraphic Corporation and moved on to involvement with many other typographic products, such as character kerning programs and founts for Apple Macintosh computer systems.

Herb Lubalin

Born 1918 in New York City. Graduated from the Cooper Union 1939. Art Director for Deutsch & Shea Advertising 1941, Fairchild Publications 1942, and Reiss Advertising 1943. Vice-president and Creative Director for Sudler & Hennessey Inc, 1945. President of Herb Lubalin Inc, 1964-67. Executive vice-president of Lubalin, Burns & Co Inc, 1967-75. Executive vice-president of the International Typeface Corporation 1971-81. Professor of Design, the Cooper Union 1976-81. He was a distinguished designer of posters, logos, magazines, advertising, packaging, books, stationery, and promotional material. Died 1981.

John Matt

Born 1940. Gained a degree in advertising and design at the Pratt Institute. After graduation entered employment with the American Type Founders Co and there began the somewhat convoluted history of Matt Antique and its derivative Garth Graphic. He worked for the Compugraphic Corporation and for RCA which was later acquired by Information International Inc. Some twenty years were spent with the latter organisation, many of them as Director of Font Development. Died 1989.

José Mendoza y Almeida

French designer of Spanish descent. Apprenticed as a photoengraver to Clichés Union in Paris, a company that adopted Monophoto filmsetting in the early days. Worked as assistant to Roger Excoffon from 1954 to 1959 at the Olive typefoundry in Marseilles, following an introduction by Maximilien Vox. Afterwards became a freelance designer and produced the type style Pascal issued by the Amsterdam foundry in 1959. His best-known typeface is Photina released by the Monotype Corporation in 1971.

Christian Mengelt

Born 1938 in Switzerland. Studied graphic design under Armin Hofmann and Emil Ruder at the School of Design, Basle. Operated own studio from 1964 and co-operated with several different design and advertising agencies, such as GCK in Basle and Mendell & Oberer in Munich. Commenced teaching of lettering and graphic design in 1972 at his alma mater. With André Gürtler and Erich Gschwind formed Team 77 and became deeply involved in most aspects of letterform design and application. Lectured at many European and American seminars in conjunction with the Association of Swiss Graphic Designers and with the ATypI Committee of Education and Research in Letterforms.

Bernd Mollenstadt

Born 1943. Studied as a compositor and graphic designer. Joined H Berthold AG in 1967 and has carried the responsibilities of its type design studio at Munich since 1968. Took charge of all Berthold fount production from 1976. Designed Formata, an exclusive sanserif family for Berthold, in 1984 and added condensed variations in 1988.

Robin Nicholas

Born 1947 in Westerham, Kent. Trained as an engineering draughtsman before joining the Monotype Typographical Drawing Office in 1965. Moved to the Typographic Design Department for the same company in 1968. Appointed Manager of the Monotype Typographical Drawing Office in 1982. In addition to creating the newspaper typeface Nimrod, Robin Nicholas has guided the development and revival of many founts between 1982 and 1989, among them Arial, Bell, Centaur, Clarion, Janson, Van Dijck, and Walbaum.

Robert Norton

Born 1929 in London. Gained a scholarship to Christ's Hospital School. First job was in the City of London with a discount house at the age of 16. Entered book publishing with Rupert Hart-Davis in 1947 and held production management positions successively with James McGivens and Vincent Stuart. Joined United Nations in New York at the time of the Suez Crisis. Went to Jamaica in 1959, taught printing and assisted in the foundation of a factory producing exercise books. Returned to the USA and worked for Cambridge University Press as a designer. Returned to the United Kingdom in 1963 and launched Photoscript Ltd, a phototypesetting trade house. He first learned to produce type founts during this period. Financial re-structuring of the company occurred in 1970 resulting in setting up of Norton Photosetting Ltd. This company was responsible for manufacturing several hundred photo-matrix founts for BobstGraphic. Set up Digital Type Systems Ltd to produce digital type founts in 1986; re-organisation of the firm led to a change in name to Digital Type Services Ltd in 1989.

Aldo Novarese

Born 1920 in Italy. Studied at the G B Paravia School of Graphic Arts in Turin. Joined the Societa Nebiolo typefoundry in 1936 and eventually became its Art Director in 1952. Collaborated with Alessandro Butti (1893-1959) on the production of a number of type designs, exemplified by Athenaeum (1945), Normandia (1946), Augustea (1951), Egizio (1956), and the titling

Microgramma (1952) to which a decade later Novarese added a lower-case alphabet and changed the name to Eurostile (1962). He was solely responsible for other designs issued by Nebiolo, including Landi (1939), Cigno (1954), Fontanesi (1954), Ritmo (1955), and Garaldus (1956). Nine designs conceived by Novarese since 1960 are shown in this book.

Friedrich Poppl

Born 1923. Studied at the State Technical College, Teplitz-Schonau in Czechoslovakia 1939-41. After war service resumed studies at the College of Applied Arts in Offenbach where Herbert Post was among the tutors. Started freelance practice as a designer 1953. Joined the teaching staff at the Wiesbaden College of Applied Arts 1962. Work exhibited widely at: Klingspor Museum, Offenbach 1961; Victoria & Albert Museum, London (Contemporary Calligraphy) 1965; Gutenburg Museum, Mainz (Lettering in Our Time) 1966; UNESCO Building, Paris (ATypI Exhibition) 1966; BMW Pavilion, Munich (ITCA Typomundus) 1969; and ITC Centre, New York (Calligraphy Today) 1980. Promoted to Senior Lecturer at Wiesbaden 1966. Signed exclusive contract with H Berthold AG for typeface design 1967; Poppl-Antiqua was the first issue from the collaboration. Recipient of the Golden Grid Award by Berthold in February 1982 not long before his death in the summer of that year.

David Quay

Born 1948. Studied graphic design at the Ravensbourne College of Art and Design. Worked for various design groups after leaving college. Decided to become a freelance lettering specialist in 1975. Established the Quay & Gray lettering design consultancy in 1983 with Paul Gray. His first typeface emerged eponymously in 1985.

John Schappler

Studied at the University of Iowa and earned a master's degree in design (1957-59). Worked for IBM in the Office Products Division on type designs for typewriters and composers with standard and proportional spacing systems (1959-65). Moved on to engagement with Graphic and Package design in Lexington, Kentucky (1965-67). Returned to lettercraft as Director of Typeface Design for the Ludlow Typograph Co (1967-71). Became Manager of Typeface Design in the Chicago office of the Compugraphic Corporation (1971-73). Appointed Director of Typography for the Sun Chemical Co (1973-76). Served with Itek Composition Systems from 1979 to 1984, initially as Manager of Typeface Design and later as Art Director.

Robert Slimbach

Born 1956 in the USA. Worked as a letter designer with Autologic Inc from 1983 to 1985, followed by two years of freelance commissions. Joined the type department of Adobe Systems Inc in 1987.

Erik Spiekermann

Born 1947. Developed an early interest in type and printing at the age of twelve with the acquisition of a Boston platen press and metal type founts of Akzidenz-Grotesk and Gill designs. Studied English and Art History at Berlin University from 1968. From 1973 worked in England as a typographer and lecturer at the London College of Printing. Later served as a freelance designer for several London agencies, such as Wolff Olins and Henrion Design Associates. He developed a close relationship at this time with H Berthold AG, adapting the established designs of Berliner Grotesk and Lo-Type. Returned to Berlin in 1983 and set up the studio MetaDesign specialising in the development of corporate identities. Author of the typographical novel *Rhyme and Reason* published in 1987.

Sumner Stone

Born 1945 in the USA. Obtained a master's degree in mathematics and later studied calligraphy with Lloyd Reynolds. First worked as a lettering artist for Hallmark Cards at a time when Hermann Zapf served as a consultant to the same company. Established his own design studio at Sonoma (California) called the Alpha and Omega Press. Entered the field of digital type design in 1979 as the Director of Typography for Autologic Inc and later for Camex Inc and for Adobe Systems Inc.

Walter Tracy

Born 1914. Apprentice compositor with William Clowes 1930-35. Typographic studio Barnard Press 1935-38 and Notley Advertising 1938-46. Worked part-time in 1947 with James Shand and Robert Harling on their publishing enterprise *Art & Technics*. Responsible for typographic development with the British arm of Linotype 1947-73 and continued in the same capacity with Linotype-Paul 1973-78. Designed several newspaper types in addition to those shown in this book, such as Jubilee (1953) and Adsans (1959). Author of *Letters of Credit: a view of type design* (1986) and *The Typographic Scene* (1988). Appointed Royal Designer for Industry in 1973 by the Royal Society of Arts.

Jan Tschichold

Born 1902 in Leipzig. Attended Academy for the Graphic Arts and Book Production in Leipzig 1919-21 and the School of Arts and Crafts in Dresden 1921. Studied under Walter Tiemann and assistant to professor Hermann Delitsch at the Leipzig Academy 1921-23. Freelance typographer and calligrapher in Leipzig 1923-25 and in Berlin 1925-26. Taught in Munich at the German Master Printers' School 1926. Publication of first book, *Die neue Typographie* 1928. Emigrated to Basle in 1933 and undertook part-time teaching at the Printing Trades School and completed commissions for the publishing house Benno Schwabe until 1940. Typographer to the publisher Birkhauser in Basle 1941-46. Implemented the typographical reform of Penguin Books in London 1946-49. Freelance designer 1950-54. Typographer to the pharmaceutical firm of F Hoffman – La Roch & Co AG 1955-67. Elected honorary Royal Designer for Industry by the Royal Society of Arts 1965. In addition to the Sabon typeface shown in this book, Tschichold designed Transito for the Amsterdam Typefoundry (1930) and Saskia for Schelter & Giesecke (1932). Died 1974.

Gerard Unger

Born 1942 in Arnhem, the Netherlands. Studied at the Rietveld Academy in Amsterdam. Worked under Wim Crouwel at an advertising agency and later at Joh Enschedé en Zonen. On becoming a freelance designer, a succession of typefaces ensued, primarily for the composition systems produced by Dr-Ing Rudolf Hell GmbH in Germany. Other work includes lettering for signs on the Amsterdam underground railway. Combines freelance work with lecturing in typography and lettering at his alma mater.

Leslie Usherwood

Born 1932. Studied at the Beckenham School of Art. Practised as a lettering artist in the commercial art field for 15 years. First typeface, called Melure, designed in 1965 for Headliners International, New York. Started Typesettra Ltd in Toronto during 1968 as a high-quality headline service with hand lettering and studio facilities. In 1972 expanded with a Berthold phototypesetting system to set advertising typography, corporate brochures, and annual reports. Several headline typefaces were conceived by Leslie Usherwood for Berthold in the early 1970s, such as Graphis Bold (1971), Statesman (1973), and Octavia (1973). Many designs ensued for bulk composition and seven are displayed in this book. By the early 1980s, Typesettra employed no fewer than four type designers. Died 1983.

Jovica Veljovic

Born 1954. Attended the Academy of Applied Arts in Belgrade and graduated in 1979. Tutored in lettering by Stjepan Fileki. First lettering book to have an influence on him was *About Alphabets* by Hermann Zapf and regular correspondence with Henri Friedlaender in Israel has been another major formative influence. Calligraphy included at the Victoria and Albert Museum in London as part of the exhibition *A Survey of Western Calligraphy from the Roman Period to 1980* and at the ITC Centre in New York as part of the review *International Calligraphy Today* in 1980. Received an award for calligraphy at the October Salon in Belgrade 1979. First typeface issued by the International Typeface Corporation in 1984.

Ong Chong Wah

Born 1955 in Malacca, Malaysia. Obtained a degree in graphic design after studies in England at Sunderland Polytechnic (1976-77) and Newcastle-upon-Tyne Polytechnic (1978-80). Worked as an Art Director for AP Saatchi & Saatchi Compton (1980-84). Later he designed the type families Footlight and Abadi for the Monotype Corporation.

Adrian Williams

Born 1950 in Bridgwater, Somerset. Attended briefly Hornsey College of Art in London. First worked for a public relations firm on house magazines and typographic layouts. Moved to Face, a trade house, as type development assistant, and undertook re-drawings of many metal alphabets for reproduction as 2-inch filmstrips. His mentor at the firm was Mike Chave and the experience provided excellent grounding in type design. Continued to work at Mushroom, a competitive trade house, for another couple of years. Operated as a freelance making founts from original designs for some eighteen months. Established the Fonts enterprise in 1974 which lasted for eleven years and saw the creation of the eight type families seen in this book. This venture was followed by the inauguration of Adrian Williams Design Ltd which produces exclusive typefaces for subscribers to the Club Type scheme. Some of the designs issued under the scheme include Column, Congress Sans, Eurocrat, Mercurius, Persidon, and Veronan.

Hermann Zapf

Born 1918 in Nuremberg. Started apprenticeship as photographic retoucher 1934 at Karl Ulrich & Co. After completion of training moved to Haus zum Fursteneck in Frankfurt and worked as lettering artist, becoming freelance 1938. First encountered punchcutting as a craft at the Stempel typefoundry just prior to 1939. Appointed artistic director by Stempel 1947. Taught at the Werkkunstschule in Offenbach 1948-50. Resigned from Stempel 1956, but continued as a consultant to the Linotype Group. Commissioned 1961 to design special type (Hunt Roman) for the Hunt Botanical Library of Carnegie Institute of Technology in Pittsburgh. Designed several types for Hallmark Cards, Kansas from 1967. Among many publications, *Manuale Typographicum* published 1954 and *About Alphabets* 1960. Thirteen type families by Hermann Zapf appear in this book, but many significant alphabets preceded 1960, instanced by Palatino (1950), Sistina Titling (1951), Melior (1952), Virtuoso (1952), Saphir (1952), Aldus (1954), and Optima (1958).

Gudrun Zapf-Von Hesse

Born 1918. Tutored by Otto Dorfner in bookbinding at Weimar. Self-taught in lettering using the manuals of Edward Johnston and Rudolf Koch, a process started in 1935 and continued in Berlin with instruction from Johannes Boehland. Designed Diotima for issue by the Stempel foundry in 1952. Smargd, an open titling, was added to the family in 1953, to be joined a year later by Ariadne (consisting of a set of swash italic capitals). Association with Hallmark Cards yielded Shakespeare roman and italic in 1968. Most recent work included Nofret for Berthold and Carmina for Bitstream, both included in this book.

Select bibliography

Association Typographique Internationale
Index of Typefaces. 1975

Bigelow, Charles; Duensing, Paul Hayden; and Gentry, Linnea (editors)
Fine Print on Type. London 1989

Biggs, John R
An Approach to Type. London 1949

Brown, Bruce
Brown's Index to Photocomposition Typography. Minehead 1983

Carter, Sebastian
Twentieth-Century Type Designers. London 1987

Craig, James
Phototypesetting: a design manual. New York 1970

Dowding, Geoffrey
Factors in the Choice of Type Faces. London 1957

Dowding, Geoffrey
Finer Points in the spacing and arrangement of type. London 1957

Dowding, Geoffrey
An Introduction to the History of Printing Types. London 1961

Frutiger, Adrian
Type Sign Symbol. Zurich 1980

Haley, Allan
Phototypography. New York 1980

Heath, Les and Faux, Ian
Phototypesetting. Manchester 1983

Hutchinson, James
Letters. London 1983

Jaspert, W Pincus; Berry, W Turner; and Johnson, A F
The Encyclopaedia of Type Faces. London 1953

Johnson, A F
Type Designs: their history and development. London 1966

Karow, Peter
Digital Formats for Typefaces. Hamburg 1987

McLean, Ruari
Typography. London 1980

Morison, Stanley
A Tally of Types. Cambridge 1953

Morison, Stanley
On Type Designs Past and Present. London 1962

Perfect, Christopher and Rookledge, Gordon
Rookledge's International Type Finder: the essential handbook of typeface recognition and selection. London 1983

Phillips, Arthur H
Handbook of Computer-Aided Composition. New York 1980

Romano, Frank J
The TypEncyclopedia: a user's guide to better typography. New York 1984

Rondthaler, Edward
Life with Letters after they Turned Photogenic. New York 1981

Ryder, John
Flowers & Flourishes. London 1976

Seybold, J W
The World of Digital Typesetting. Media 1984

Spencer, Herbert
The Visible Word. London 1968

Spencer, Herbert
Pioneers of Modern Typography. London 1969

Sutton, James and Bartram, Alan
An Atlas of Typeforms. London 1968

Sutton, James and Bartram, Alan
Typefaces for Books. London 1990

Tracy, Walter
Letters of Credit. London 1986

Tracy, Walter
The Typographic Scene. London 1988

Updike, Daniel Berkeley
Printing Types their history, forms and use. Cambridge (USA) 1937

Wallis, L W
Electronic Typesetting: a quarter century of technological upheaval. London 1984 (available from John Taylor Book Ventures)

Wallis, L W
Type Design Developments 1970-1985. Arlington 1985 (available from Keith Hogg Bookseller, Tenterden, Kent)

Wallis, L W
A Concise Chronology of Typesetting Developments 1886-1986. London 1988

Wheatley, W F
Typeface Analogue. Arlington 1988

Zapf, Hermann
About Alphabets: some marginal notes on type design. Cambridge (USA) 1970

Chronological index

1982
Beatrice Script
WTC Carnase Text
Catull
Certificate Face Bold
Cosmos
Cremona
Criterion
ITC Cushing
Devendra
Else
ITC Galliard (originated in 1978)
WTC Goudy
Imago
ITC Modern 216
ITC New Baskerville
Poppl-Laudatio
Poppl-Nero
Rainbow Bass
Shannon
WTC Thaddeus
Vario
Versailles
Weinz Kurvalin

1983
AG Schulbuch
Barmen
ITC Berkeley Old Style
Bodoni Old Face
Bryn Mawr
ITC Caslon 224
Clarion
Delta
Edwardian
Expert
Feinan
Hollander
Marbrook
Neue Helvetica
Proteus
Trieste
ITC Weidemann

1984
AG Old Face
Colossal
Draco
Formata
Franco
Henche
Jaeger-Antiqua
LCD
Neue Luthersche Fraktur
Osiris
Pictor

Sayer Esprit
ITC Symbol
ITC Usherwood
Vela
ITC Veljovic

1985
AG Buch Stencil
Aurelia
Certificate Face Bold
Champfleury
Daily News
ITC Elan
ITC Esprit
WTC Favrile
Geometrica
Isadora
Janson Text
Jersey
Kis-Janson
ITC Leawood
Lucida
Melencolia
ITC Mixage
Quay
Swift

1986
Bellevue
Boton
Cantoria
Linotype Centennial
Bitstream Cooper
WTC Cursivium
Epikur
Footlight
ITC Gamma
ITC Goudy Sans
Guardi
Hiroshige
Mainorm
Nofret
Schuller

1987
Abadi
Bitstream Amerigo
Calisto
Bitstream Carmina
Bitstream Charter
Gerstner Original
Lucida Bright
WTC Neufont
ITC Pacella
Schneider-Antiqua
ITC Slimbach

Stone Informal
Stone Sans
Stone Serif
ITC Tiepolo
Woop De Doo Bold
Zapf Renaissance

1988
Arial
Avantis
Avenir
Chasseur
ITC Jamille
Kursivschrift
ITC Panache
WTC Veritas
Visigoth
Wilke

1989
Amigo
Arbiter
Arena (now called Stadia)
Black White
Campanile (previously Avanti)
Adobe Charlemagne
Compus
Cornet
Adobe Cottonwood
Cyrano
Dalcora
Adobe Garamond
ITC Giovanni
ITC Golden Type
Helicon
Industria
Adobe Lithos
Majora
Marigold
Mikaway
Mirarae
Monti
WTC Our Bodoni
Oxford
Pelican
PE Proforma
Rotis Semi Sans
Rotis Serif
Rotis Semi Serif
Sierra
Sympathie
Today Sans Serif
Adobe Trajan
Adobe Utopia

1990
Agora
Adobe Cottonwood
Ellington
Galathea
Adobe Ironwood
Adobe Juniper
Adobe Mesquite
Adobe Minion
Adobe Ponderosa
ITC Quay Sans
PE Scherzo
Adobe Tekton
Vergil
Wile Roman

Index of designers

Bernie Abel
Abel Cursive

Otl Aicher
Rotis Semi Sans
Rotis Serif
Rotis Semi Serif

Vladimir Andrich
Allan
American Gothic
Beatrice Script
Contempo
Cremona
Magna Carta
Vladimir

Ronald Arnholm
WTC Veritas

Arthur Baker
Amigo
Marigold
Oxford
Pelican
Visigoth

Ray Baker
ITC Newtext
ITC Quorum

Manfred Barz
Quadriga-Antiqua

Saul Bass
Rainbow Bass

Konrad Bauer
Impressum (with Walter Baum)

Walter Baum
Impressum (with Konrad Bauer)

Russell Bean
Washington

Georg Belwe
Belwe

Edward Benguiat
ITC Barcelona
ITC Bauhaus (with Victor Caruso)
ITC Benguiat
ITC Benguiat Gothic
ITC Bookman
ITC Caslon 224

ITC Korinna (with Victor Caruso)
ITC Modern 216
ITC Panache
ITC Souvenir
ITC Tiffany

Charles Bigelow
Lucida (with Kris Holmes)
Lucida Bright (with Kris Holmes)

W Bilz
Life (with F Simoncini)

Constance Blanchard
Garth Graphic (with Renée Le Winter)

Ronne Bonder
ITC Gorilla (with Tom Carnase)
ITC Grizzly (with Tom Carnase)
ITC Grouch (with Tom Carnase)
ITC Honda (with Tom Carnase)
ITC Machine (with Tom Carnase)
ITC Milano Roman (with Tom Carnase)
ITC Pioneer (with Tom Carnase)
ITC Tom's Roman (with Tom Carnase)

Jelle Bosma
WTC Cursivium

Albert Boton
Agora
Boton
ITC Elan
ITC Eras (with Albert Hollenstein)
PE Scherzo

Chris Brand
Albertina

George Brian
Souvenir Gothic

Alan Bright
Brighton

Colin Brignall
Aachen
Corinthian
Edwardian
Italia
Revue
Romic

Neville Brody
Arena (now called Stadia)
Campanile (previously Avanti)
Industria

Jackson Burke
Aurora

Margaret Calvert
Calvert

Jerry Campbell
ITC Isbell (with Richard Isbell)

Tom Carnase
ITC Avant Garde Gothic (with Herb Lubalin)
WTC Carnase Text
WTC Favrile
ITC Gorilla (with Ronne Bonder)
WTC Goudy
ITC Grizzly (with Ronne Bonder)
ITC Grouch (with Ronne Bonder)
ITC Honda (with Ronne Bonder)
ITC Machine (with Ronne Bonder)
ITC Milano Roman (with Ronne Bonder)
WTC Our Bodoni (with Massimo Vignelli)
ITC Pioneer (with Ronne Bonder)
ITC Tom's Roman (with Ronne Bonder)

Ron Carpenter
Calisto
Cantoria

Matthew Carter
Auriga
Bell Centennial
Cascade Script
Bitstream Charter
Cochin
ITC Galliard
Gando Ronde (with Hans-Jorg Hunziker)
Olympian
Shelley Script
Snell Roundhand
Video

Will Carter
Octavian (with David Kindersley)

Victor Caruso
ITC Bauhaus (with Edward Benguiat)
ITC Clearface
ITC Franklin Gothic
ITC Korinna (with Edward Benguiat)

Joseph Churchward
Churchward 69
Churchward 70

Mike Daines
University

Carl Dair
Cartier

Bram de Does
Trinité

Antonio DiSpigna
ITC Serif Gothic (with Herb Lubalin)

Dick Dooijes
Contura
Lectura

Ferdinay Duman
Black White
Compus
Majora
Sympathie

Sigrid Engelmann
ITC Golden Type
(with Helge Jorgensen and
Andrew Newton)

Roger Excoffon
Antique Olive

Erich Fehrle
Fehrle Display

Ernst Friz
Friz Quadrata

Adrian Frutiger
Apollo
Avenir
Breughel
Linotype Centennial
Frutiger
Glypha
Icone
Iridium
OCR B
Serifa
Tiemann
(adapted from the work of Walter
Tiemann)
Versailles

Marco Ganz
Avantis

Karl Gerstner
Gerstner Original

Barbara Gibb
Vela

Frederic W Goudy
ITC Goudy Sans

Erich Gschwind
Media
(with André Gürtler and Christian Mengelt)
Signa
(with André Gürtler and Christian Mengelt)
Haas Unica
(with André Gürtler and Christian Mengelt)

André Gürtler
Basilia
Egyptian 505
Media
(with Christian Mengelt and Erich Gschwind)
Signa
(with Christian Mengelt and Erich Gschwind)
Haas Unica
(with Christian Mengelt and Erich Gschwind)

Michael Harvey
Ellington

Reinhard Haus
Guardi

Hans Heitmann
Galathea

Linda Hoffman
Cloe
Franco

Dieter Hofrichter
Vergil

Hollis Holland
Holland Seminar

Cynthia Hollandsworth
Hiroshige
Wile Roman

Albert Hollenstein
ITC Eras (with Albert Boton)

Kris Holmes
Isadora
Lucida (with Charles Bigelow)
Lucida Bright (with Charles Bigelow)
Shannon (with Janice Prescott)
Sierra

Hans-Jorg Hunziker
Gando Ronde (with Matthew Carter)

Richard Isbell
Americana
ITC Isbell (with Jerry Campbell)

Gustav Jaeger
Aja
Bellevue
Catull
Chasseur
Cornet
Cosmos
Daily News
Delta
Epikur
Jaeger-Antiqua
Jersey
Jumbo
Osiris
Seneca

Mark Jamra
ITC Jamille

Wulf Jarosche
Kapitellia
Napoleon

Helge Jorgensen
ITC Golden Type
(with Sigrid Engelmann and Andrew Newton)

Dick Jones
Crillee

Joel Kadan
ITC American Typewriter (with Tony Stan)

Ed Kelton
Helserif

David Kindersley
Itek Bookface
Octavian (with Will Carter)

Erwin Koch
Dalcora
Monanti
Monti

Georg Kuhn
Las Vegas

Volker Kuster
Neue Luthersche Fraktur
Today Sans Serif

Frederick Lambert
Compacta

Günter Gerhard Lange
AG Buch Stencil
AG Old Face
Baskerville Book
Berthold Script
Bodoni Old Face
Caslon Buch
Concorde
Concorde Nova
El Greco
Franklin Antiqua
Garamond
Imago
Walbaum Buch
Walbaum Standard

Rick Lawrie
Certificate Face Bold

Joffre Lefevre
Draco

Renée le Winter
Garth Graphic (with Constance Blanchard)

Herb Lubalin
ITC Avant Garde Gothic (with Tom Carnase)
ITC Lubalin Graph
ITC Serif Gothic (with Antonio DiSpigna)

Karlheinz Maireder
Mainorm

Phil Martin
Adroit
Bluejack
Criterion
Heldustry
Martin Gothic

John Matt
Matt Antique

Alan Meeks
Bramley
Plaza

Hans E Meier
Syntax

José Mendoza y Almeida
Photina

Christian Mengelt
Media
(with André Gürtler and Erich Gschwind)
Signa
(with André Gürtler and Erich Gschwind)
Haas Unica
(with André Gürtler and Erich Gschwind)

Kazimierz Mika
Mikaway

Henry Mikiewicz
Feinan

Bernd Mollenstadt
Formata

Andrew Newton
ITC Golden Type
(with Sigrid Engelmann and Helge Jorgenen)

Chew Loon Ng
Accolade

Robin Nicholas
Nimrod

Robert Norton
Else

Aldo Novarese
Arbiter
Colossal
Eurostile
Expert
ITC Fenice
Lapidar
ITC Mixage
ITC Novarese
ITC Symbol

Vincent Pacella
ITC Cushing
ITC Pacella

John Peters
Fleet Titling
Traveller

Erwin Poell
Poell

Friedrich Poppl
Poppl-Antiqua
Poppl-College
Poppl-Exquisit
Poppl-Laudatio
Poppl-Nero
Poppl-Pontifex
Poppl-Residenz

Janice Prescott
Shannon (with Kris Holmes)

David Quay
Helicon
Quay
ITC Quay Sans

Hans Reichel
Barmen

Arthur Ritzel
Rotation

Freda Sack
Proteus
Stratford (with Adrian Williams)

Friedrich Karl Sallwey
Present

Manfred Sayer
Sayer Esprit

John Schappler
PaulMark
RitaScript

Werner Schneider
Schneider-Antiqua

Manfred H Schuller
Schuller

David Siegel
Adobe Tekton

F Simoncini
Life (with W Bilz)

Robert Slimbach
Adobe Garamond
ITC Giovanni
Adobe Minion
ITC Slimbach
Adobe Utopia

Erik Spiekermann
Berliner Grotesk
Lo-Type

Tony Stan
ITC American Typewriter (with Joel Kadan)
ITC Berkeley Old Style
ITC Century
ITC Cheltenham
ITC Garamond

Robert Stefanic
Henche
Woop De Doo Bold

E Strohm
Itek Blackletter

Sumner Stone
Stone Formal
Stone Sans
Stone Serif

Thaddeus Szumilas
WTC Thaddeus

D Thaker
Devendra

Walter Tiemann
Tiemann (adapted by Adrian Frutiger)

Walter Tracy
Maximus
Modern
Times Europa

Joseph Treacy
Bryn Mawr

Jan Tschichold
Sabon

Carol Twombly
Adobe Charlemagne
Adobe Lithos
Mirarae
Adobe Trajan

Gerard Unger
Bitstream Amerigo
Cyrano
Demos
Flora
Hollander
Praxis
Swift

Leslie Usherwood
Administer
Caxton
Flange
ITC Leawood
Lynton
Marbrook
ITC Usherwood

Petr van Blokland
PE Proforma

Jovica Veljovic
ITC Esprit
ITC Gamma
ITC Veljovic

Massimo Vignelli
WTC Our Bodoni (with Tom Carnase)

Ong Chong Wah
Abadi
Footlight

Kurt Weidemann
ITC Weidemann

David Weinz
WTC Neufont
Weinz Kurvalin

Martin Wilke
Wilke

Adrian Williams
Claridge
Congress
Leamington
Raleigh
Seagull
Stratford (with Freda Sack)
Trieste
Worcester Round

Gudrun Zapf-Von Hesse
Bitstream Carmina
Nofret

Hermann Zapf
Aurelia
Comenius
Edison
Marconi
Medici Script
Noris Script
Orion
Vario
Venture Script
ITC Zapf Book
ITC Zapf Chancery
ITC Zapf International
Zapf Renaissance

Index of manufacturers and design agencies

(Ownership rights)

Adobe
Adobe Charlemagne
Adobe Cottonwood
Adobe Garamond
Adobe Ironwood
Adobe Juniper
Adobe Lithos
Adobe Mesquite
Adobe Minion
Adobe Ponderosa
Adobe Stone Informal
Adobe Stone Sans
Adobe Stone Serif
Adobe Tekton
Adobe Trajan
Adobe Utopia

Alphabet Innovations
Bluejack
Helserif
Martin Gothic

AlphaOmega Typography
Amigo
Hiroshige
Marigold
Oxford
Pelican
Visigoth
Wile Roman

Alphatype
Allan
American Gothic
Beatrice Script
Contempo
Cremona
Magna Carta
Vladimir

American Type Founders
Americana

Autologic
Champfleury
Geometrica
Kis-Janson
Media
Melencolia
Signa
Trinité

Bauer (Neufville)
Impressum
Serifa

Berthold
AG Buch Stencil
AG Old Face
AG Schulbuch
Agora
Aja
Arbiter
Avantis
Barmen
Baskerville Book
Bellevue
Berliner Grotesk
Berthold Script
Bodoni Old Face
Boton
Caslon Buch
Catull
Chasseur
Colossal
Comenius
Concorde
Concorde Nova
Cornet
Cosmos
Daily News
Delta
El Greco
Englische Schreibschrift
Epikur
Formata
Franklin Antiqua
Galathea
Garamond
Gerstner Original
Helicon
Imago
Jaeger-Antiqua
Jersey
Jumbo
Kursivschrift
Lapidar
LCD
Lo-Type
Mainorm
Marbrook
Mikaway
Nofret
Osiris
Poell
Poppl-Antiqua
Poppl-College
Poppl-Exquisit
Poppl-Laudatio
Poppl-Nero
Poppl-Pontifex

Poppl-Residenz
Quadriga-Antiqua
Sayer Esprit
Schneider-Antiqua
Schuller
Seneca
Vergil
Walbaum Buch
Walbaum Standard

Bigelow & Holmes
Lucida
Lucida Bright

Bitstream
Bitstream Amerigo
Bitstream Carmina
Bitstream Charter
Bitstream Cooper

Churchward International
Churchward 69
Churchward 70

**Compugraphic
(Agfa Corporation)**
Abel Cursive
Draco
Feinan
Garth Graphic
Holland Seminar
Pictor
Rotis Semi Sans
Rotis Serif
Rotis Semi Serif
Shannon
Uncle Sam
Vela

Fonts/Ingrama SA
Accolade
Claridge
Congress
Leamington
Raleigh
Seagull
Stratford
Trieste
Worcester Round

Haas
Basilia
Expert
Haas Unica

Hell
Aurelia
Black White
Compus
Cyrano
Dalcora
Demos
Digi-Grotesk Series S
Edison
Flora
Hollander
Isadora
Kapitellia
Majora
Marconi
Monanti
Monti
Napoleon
Praxis
Sierra
Swift
Sympathie
Vario

International Typeface Corporation
ITC American Typewriter
ITC Avant Garde Gothic
ITC Barcelona
ITC Bauhaus
ITC Benguiat
ITC Benguiat Gothic
ITC Berkeley Old Style
ITC Bookman
ITC Caslon 224
ITC Century
ITC Cheltenham
ITC Clearface
ITC Cushing
ITC Elan
ITC Eras
ITC Esprit
ITC Fenice
ITC Franklin Gothic
Friz Quadrata
ITC Galliard
ITC Gamma
ITC Garamond
ITC Giovanni
ITC Golden Type
ITC Gorilla
ITC Goudy Sans
ITC Grizzly
ITC Grouch
ITC Honda
ITC Isbell

Italia
ITC Jamille
ITC Kabel
ITC Korinna
ITC Leawood
ITC Lubalin Graph
ITC Machine
ITC Milano Roman
ITC Mixage
ITC Modern 216
ITC New Baskerville
ITC Newtext
ITC Novarese
ITC Pacella
ITC Panache
ITC Pioneer
ITC Quay Sans
ITC Quorum
ITC Serif Gothic
ITC Slimbach
ITC Souvenir
ITC Symbol
ITC Tiepolo
ITC Tiffany
ITC Tom's Roman
ITC Usherwood
ITC Veljovic
ITC Weidemann
ITC Zapf Book
ITC Zapf Chancery
ITC Zapf International

Itek
Itek Blackletter
Itek Bookface
Certificate Face Bold
Matt Antique
PaulMark
RitaScript
Weinz Kurvalin

Letraset
Aachen
Bramley
Brighton
Caxton
Compacta
Corinthian
Crillee
Edwardian
Plaza
Proteus
Quay
Revue
Romic
University
Zipper

Lettergietterij Amsterdam
Contura
Lectura

Linotype
Arena (now called Stadia)
Auriga

Aurora
Avenir
Breughel
Bryn Mawr
Campanile (previously Avanti)
Cascade Script
Linotype Centennial
Cochin
Devendra
Fehrle Display
Frutiger
Gando Ronde
Glypha
Guardi
Hanseatic
Helvetica Rounded
Icone
Industria
Iridium
Janson Text
Las Vegas
Maximus
Medici Script
Modern
Neue Helvetica
Neuzeit S
New Caledonia
Noris Script
Olympian
Orion
Present
Rainbow Bass
Rotation
Shelley Script
Snell Roundhand
Syntax
Tiemann
Times Europa
Venture Script
Versailles
Video
Linotype Walbaum
Wilke

Ludwig & Mayer
Permanent Headline

Monotype
Abadi
Albertina
Apollo
Arial
Calisto
Calvert
Cantoria
Clarion
Ellington
Fleet Titling
Footlight
Nimrod
Octavian
Photina
Traveller

Morisawa
Mirarae

Nebiolo
Eurostile

Norton Photosetting
Else

Olive
Antique Olive

Purup Electronics
PE Proforma
PE Scherzo

Scangraphic
Neue Luthersche Fraktur
Today Sans Serif
Zapf Renaissance

Schelter & Giesecke
Belwe

Simoncini
Life

Type Designers International
Washington

Typesettra
Administer
Flange
Lynton

TypeSpectra
Adroit
Criterion
Heldustry
Souvenir Gothic

Varityper
Cloe
Franco
Henche
Woop De Doo Bold

Visual Graphics Corporation
Cartier
Egyptian 505

World Typeface Center
WTC Carnase Text
WTC Cursivium
WTC Favrile
WTC Goudy
WTC Neufont
WTC Our Bodoni
WTC Thaddeus
WTC Veritas

Index of alternative typeface names

Derived name	Original name
AG	ITC Avant Garde Gothic
AG Buch Rounded	Helvetica Rounded
Aldine 701	ITC Galliard
Aldine 851	ITC Garamond
Aldostyle	Eurostile
AM	Americana
American Classic	Americana
AO	Antique Olive
AT	ITC American Typewriter
Berner	Sabon
BG	ITC Benguiat
BH	ITC Bauhaus
BM	ITC Bookman
Brunswick	Poppl-Pontifex
BT	ITC Benguiat Gothic
BY	ITC Berkeley Old Style
Calligraphic 750	Seagull
Calligraphic 816	Caxton
Century 711	ITC Century
CF	ITC Clearface
CG Collage	Cochin
CG Triumvirate No.2	Neue Helvetica
CH	ITC Cheltenham
Chancery 801	ITC Zapf Chancery
Charlemagne	Aachen
Chinchilla	Concorde
Cintal	Syntax
CJ	Concorde
Classical Garamond	Sabon
Colonial	Americana
Copperplate 421	ITC Newtext
Copperplate 701	ITC Serif Gothic
Copperplate 721	ITC Symbol
Cosimo Script	Medici Script
Decorated 081	ITC Pioneer
Dutch 791	ITC Grouch
Dutch Roman	Holland Seminar

Derived name	Original name
EE	Else
Egypt 55	Egyptian 505
Egyptios	Egyptian 505
EI	ITC Elan
Elliptical 716	ITC Zapf Book
Elliptical 717	ITC Zapf International
Empira	Aurora
English 111	Shelley Script
English 401	Snell Roundhand
English Script	Englische Schreibschrift
Engravers Roundhand	Snell Roundhand
EP	ITC Esprit
ER	ITC Eras
ES	Eurostile
Europa Grotesk No.2	Neue Helvetica
FE	ITC Fenice
Flareserif 721	Americana
Flareserif 816	Fritz Quadrata
Flareserif 851	ITC Quorum
Fredonia	Life
Freeborn	Frutiger
Freedom	Americana
Freeform 731	ITC Souvenir
Freehand 471	Cascade Script
French 111	Gando Ronde
Frontiera	Frutiger
FZ	Fritz Quadrata
GA	ITC Gamma
Gail Script	Noris Script
Geneva 2	Neue Helvetica
Geneva Roundhand	Helvetica Rounded
Gentleman	Glypha
Geometric 711	ITC Avant Garde Gothic
Geometric 731	ITC Kabel
Geometric 735	ITC Grizzly
Geometric 752	ITC Bauhaus
Geometric Slabserif 761	ITC Lubalin Graph
GI	ITC Garamond
GL	ITC Galliard
GN	ITC Goudy Sans
Gothic 744	ITC Franklin Gothic

Gothic 762	Bell Centennial	*Revival 425*	ITC Gorilla
Grotesk S	Neuzeit S	*Revival 711*	ITC Bookman
Helios Rounded	Helvetica Rounded	*Revival 721*	ITC Cushing
Helvetica No.2	Neue Helvetica	*Revival 758*	Tom's Roman
Humanist 777	Frutiger	*Revival 791*	Italia
Humanist 785	ITC Mixage	*Revival 814*	ITC Clearface
HV	Neue Helvetica	*Revival 821*	ITC Isbell
Incised 726	ITC Eras	*Revival 831*	ITC Tiffany
Incised 901	Antique Olive	*Revival 832*	ITC Benguiat
Industrial 817	ITC Fenice	*Revival 851*	University
Informal 851	ITC Benguiat Gothic	*RH*	Snell Roundhand
Informal 870	Revue	*Riga*	Auriga
Iron	Iridium	*Rotieren*	Rotation
IS	ITC Isbell	*Sandpiper*	Seagull
IT	Italia	*September*	Sabon
Kaskade Script	Cascade Script	*Seraphim*	Serifa
KL	ITC Kabel	*Seriverse*	Serifa
KN	ITC Korinna	*SG*	ITC Serif Gothic
Latin 671	ITC Novarese	*Siegfried*	Frutiger
LE	Lectura	*Signet Roundhand*	Snell Roundhand
LG	ITC Lubalin Graph	*SL*	ITC Slimbach
Microstyle	Eurostile	*Square 721*	Eurostile
News No.2	Aurora	*Square 880*	ITC Machine
News No.12	Aurora	*Stubserif 705*	ITC Cheltenham
News 706	Aurora	*Stubserif 711*	ITC Korinna
NO	ITC Novarese	*SV*	ITC Souvenir
Norris Script	Noris Script	*Swiss 930*	Compacta
NT	ITC Newtext	*Swiss Slabserif 722*	Serifa
Oliva	Antique Olive	*SX*	Syntax
Olive	Antique Olive	*Sybil*	Sabon
Operinia	Shelley Script	*Symphony*	Syntax
PC	ITC Pacella	*Symposia*	Sabon
Penman Script	Snell Roundhand	*Synchron*	Syntax
Pharaoh	Glypha	*Synthesis*	Syntax
Power	Poppl-Pontifex	*Transport*	Concorde
Provencale	Frutiger	*Traverse*	Cochin
QM	ITC Quorum	*TY*	ITC Tiffany
		Typewriter 911	ITC American Typewriter
		UY	University
		Venetian 519	ITC Berkeley Old Style
		Ventura	Venture Script
		ZC	ITC Zapf Chancery
		ZF	ITC Zapf Book